The Age of the
AUTOMOBILE

Merry Christmas Matt
from Grandma & Grandpa Galeazzi
1978

Merry Christmas Matt
from Grandma & Grandpa Galeazzi
1978

The Age of the
AUTOMOBILE
George Bishop

HAMLYN
London·New York·Sydney·Toronto

Acknowledgements

The publishers are grateful to the following individuals and organizations for the illustrations in this book: Alfa Romeo; Audi NSU; *Autocar*; Automobile Association; Automobile Manufacturers' Association; Hugh W. Bishop; BMW; Michael Boys; British Leyland; Neill Bruce; W. J. Brunell; Chrysler; Citroën; Colt; Michael Cooper; Daimler-Benz; Ferodo; Fiat; Ford; The Henry Ford Museum; General Motors; Geoffrey Goddard; Ray Hutton; David Hodges Collection; Indianapolis Motor Speedway; Jaguar; Leigh Jones; Lancia; London Transport; Lotus; Ozzie Lyons; Mazda; Michelin; Morgan; *Motor*; Musée de l'Automobile de Mans; Nationaal Foto Persbureau; National Motor Museum; Opel; Phipps Photographic; Pictorial Press; Pirelli; Planet News; Charles Pocklington; Polski Car Imports; Press Association; Radio Times Hulton Picture Library; Reliant; Rolls-Royce; Rover; Saab; Satra Motors; The Science Museum; Shell; Skoda; Jerry Sloniger; Nigel Snowdon; Jasper Spencer-Smith; Swiss Museum of Transport and Communications; Colin Taylor; *Thoroughbred & Classic Car*; Vauxhall; H. Roger Viollet; Volkswagen; Volvo; David Burgess Wise; C. H. Wood; Nick Wright.

Published by The Hamlyn Publishing Group Limited
London · New York · Sydney · Toronto
Astronaut House, Feltham, Middlesex, England
Copyright © The Hamlyn Publishing Group Limited 1977

ISBN 0 600 30319 5

Printed in Great Britain
by Jarrold and Sons Limited, Norwich

Contents

The Formative Years

The motor car is very much a United Nations achievement. No one man can say 'alone I did it': it was invented by the Germans, made practical by the French and first produced on a massive scale by the Americans. The English lagged behind in the early days but caught up in the early years of the 20th Century to contribute some honoured names, now mostly dead and forgotten except by those fanatics who worship at the shrine of the automobile.

It has been with us as a practical, useable everyday device since about the turn of the century, although one can argue about exactly when it ceased to be a toy of the rich and became a tool of everyman's trade. Some of the most honoured and revered names belong to men who only produced a few machines, fewer in a lifetime than a firm like Ford make in one day. Yet their names linger on as the canonized saints of the automobile world. Why?

If we drive today the machines they made many years ago it is hard to find the magic, which has long been exorcised by precision machine tools able to work to a greater degree of accuracy than any craftsman. When the old-car fanatic says, 'They don't build 'em like that any more,' the experienced mechanic will say, 'Thank God', because he knows the problem of trying to improve minimal braking power to a standard it was never intended to produce, and of hours of dismantling to reach the heart of an ancient mechanism and replace a minor part which has failed.

So let us not delude ourselves about the qualities of the ancients, much as we may love them. Ettore Bugatti, one of the automotive saints, was honest about the faults of his beautifully-made cars. When people complained about the brakes he said, 'My cars were made to go, not to stop,' and if the question of difficult starting in cold weather was raised his answer was, 'A gentleman should have a heated motor-house'.

Whether or not he ever did say these things can be argued until the horses come home; certain facets of motoring are agreed among historians, but about many others arguments are still raging about who stole what design ideas from whom 70 or 80 years ago, and are never likely to be resolved. So we tread on thin ice when we say categorically that Benz did this and Daimler did that.

Although the effective motor car is a child of the 20th Century, the first machine which moved on wheels under its own power goes back about 200 years to Joseph Cugnot, working in France,

above
The De Dion steam tricycle of 1894 shows how far we have come from the pioneer days of toil and trouble. What a frightening device this must have been from a horse's point of view

left
One hundred years before the first motor car, Cugnot produced this massive steam carriage of 1770 for moving artillery pieces. It is now in a Paris museum, and frightening to behold

This early steam-driven equippage, complete with small boy to stoke the boiler, was built by Crompton in India in the 1860s.

A licensed artist's impression of the Enterprise steam omnibus which the London and Paddington Steam Carriage Company began operating in April 1833. It was built for them by the celebrated Mr Walter Hancock of Stratford

but said by some to be Swiss, who fabricated a steam-driven cart to carry big guns. His first effort could run for about a quarter of an hour at three miles an hour with four people aboard and presumably a gun, since that was the object of the exercise. A second edition made about ten years later in 1770 or so still exists in the Paris Conservatoire des Arts et Métiers museum. It is an enormous tricycle with wooden wheels made so that the engine and boiler turned with the front wheel, and a pretty remote ancestor to any motor car as we now know it.

Steam was the power source of those days, but the problem was to produce enough steam without the boiler being too big and heavy to be portable, and there was a lull of 30 years or so until the early 1800s when at least one steam carriage actually carried people on the road. The designer's name is familiar: Richard Trevithick, a Cornish engineer. He upped the speed to 12 miles an hour with eight people in a closed box like the centre part of a horse-drawn carriage with the driver perched out in front like a coachman.

Trevithick's London Road Carriage of 1803 used a high-pressure 60 lb boiler, which inspired many others to have a go at steam-driven road coaches, while he abandoned the idea and turned to other things. The boiler remained the key problem, although by 1841 the Summers and Ogle coach used 250 lb pressure and achieved 32 miles an hour and another of different make ran 128 miles in a day. Inevitably a boiler exploded (in 1834) to produce the first fatal road accident with a self-propelled vehicle, at Paisley in Scotland when five people were killed as John Scott Russell's machine disintegrated.

Famous names among the steam coach men were Sir Goldsworthy Gurney, who ran a regular service from Cheltenham to Gloucester, and R. W. Thompson, whose tractor-and-trailer design was the first road vehicle to run on rubber tyres, in the year 1867. Walter Hancock, whose run was between Paddington and the City in London, even made money from his operations.

But all the people who were making money from the horse-drawn stage coaches ganged up to oppose the new-fangled steamers, and the owners of the privately-built turnpike roads put up their charges to an unsupportable level. Drivers and firemen were beaten up by hired thugs, and the steam coach era came to an end.

Steam had a revival in the early days of the petrol-driven car, but eventually faded away, although Leyland Cars still have an experimental engine with which Sir Alec Issigonis was involved. Steam's rivals came on the scene as early as 1860 when Ettienne Lenoir patented a gas-driven engine, and by 1876 Doctor N. A. Otto had evolved the gas engine with a four-stroke cycle to which his name has stuck even since.

Nothing new under the sun? The Citroën 2CV was not the first car made of corrugated sheeting, witness the roof of this steam carriage built in 1885 by James Summer of Leyland for Carlisle biscuit-maker Theodore Carr

It looks as if they have just taken the horse away for the night—this Delahaye was a true horseless carriage with an engine under the rear seat and chain drive to the wooden cart wheels

The railways, which were booming in the mid-19th Century, also played their part as steam designers turned to rail locomotives rather than road ones, and the iron road began to offer cheap and predictable travel to the masses while the idea of independent private journeys remained the province of the rich. As early as 1860 another blow to the idea of the motor car was struck in England when Parliament decreed that mechanical vehicles of any kind must have a crew of three, one of whom should walk in front carrying a red flag, and that speed should be limited to four miles a hour on the open road and two miles an hour in towns.

This was the first official strangulation of the private vehicle idea, and gave the go-ahead to Continental designers while the English held back. As the end of the 19th Century approached so did the forerunners of what we now know as the motor car, although the name then appropriately enough was horseless carriage. They simply failed to harness the horses, left off the shafts, and tied the crude engine on somehow and coupled it to the wheels.

Dr Otto was mentioned earlier. On his staff was Gottlieb Daimler, a pioneer whose name survives as a car marque today in England as well as in his native Germany. He was born in 1834, ten years earlier than the other Father of the Motor Car, Karl Benz. Both men came from the same area and both were employed, at different times, in the same works (Maschinenbau-Gesellschaft, Karlsruhe), yet they never met.

They were completely opposed in temperament. Benz, although a pioneer inventor and arguably producer of the first car, was conservative and kept on making his old-fashioned cars more or less unchanged for 15 years until no-one would buy them. About the only concession was to switch from three wheels to four. Karl Benz, son of a Mannheim engine driver, is said to have been bitten by the mechanical bug when still at school, and to have imitated the motions of a connecting rod with his father's walking stick. There is certainly nobody alive today who can deny that story!

Benz talked his mother into sending him to technical school, then to the Karlsruhe locomotive parts shop. Later he formed his own company to make small gas engines, but was 38 years old when he first drove his tricycle at 10 miles an hour in the streets of Mannheim. Although ten years younger than Daimler he remained the stick-in-the-mud of the two, although he did use the new electric-spark ignition when Daimler stuck to the old-style 'hot tube' – which was just that, a piece of pipe stuck in the cylinder and heated at the outside end.

Daimler began with a motor bicycle, but was 51 when he produced it. He had been making gas engines for more than a dozen years though, and quit the Deutz works run by Otto and Langen in 1882 to make his own smaller engines, persuading his colleague Wilhelm Maybach – another pioneer name – to go with him. Daimler's motor bike emerged in 1885, the same year as the Benz tricycle, and the motor-driven carriages followed, so the two great men were working neck and neck.

But Daimler was more flexible and open to ideas. Benz put his engine at the back of his car with a horizontal flywheel which he thought more stable. Daimler tried both rear and front-mounted engines. Even his first engine had an enclosed crank and flywheel and ran up to 750 rpm, an enormous speed compared with the 150 or so which the old stationary engines could achieve. Daimler's engines were bought in large numbers by the French pioneers – Panhard, Levassor, Peugeot – for use in their own cars.

Once the car had been seen to work the next step inevitably was that people began to challenge each other to races, particularly in France which was the birthplace of motor racing. They began as early as 1894, and it was the competition between marques which forced the pace of development. Engines became faster running and more reliable, control systems improved, as did steering, suspension, roadholding, brakes, and every aspect of the horseless carriage.

below
The very first Benz, or how pollution began. Odd to modern eyes are the horizontal flywheel – it was thought that a vertical one would cause gyroscopic problems – and the way all the works are in the fresh air

left
The first Daimler of 1886 which is interesting to compare with the first Benz. Both are obviously carts put before the horse as it were, with rear engines, but in different places

Steering was the first major problem to rear its head. Carriages traditionally had a single pivot in the middle of the front axle, but this would not do at the greater speeds of the mechanically-propelled vehicle. The pioneers tried to dodge the problem by using a single front wheel, although Rudoph Ackermann had patented his idea of using independent pivots for each front wheel and tying them together with a rod, back in 1818. He had borrowed the notion from Lenkensperger who thought of it even earlier, and there is even a precedent some 200 years back which had been quite forgotten.

But what we now know as the Ackermann principle finally solved Benz's problem in 1890, and enabled the four-wheeler to take over from the tricycle without the instability problems which beset the earliest vehicles. Daimler had used four wheels from the start.

The first long-distance ride was made on a Benz in 1888, when Karl's wife and sons Eugen, 15, and Richard, 13, took off one summer night without his knowledge to visit grandfather at Pforzheim. They bought motor spirit from the chemist, had blacksmiths take up the slack in the chains, cobblers reline the crude brake shoes with leather.

Frau Benz cleared a clogged fuel-line with a hairpin and used one of her garters as insulating tape to cure an electrical short. On arrival they proudly sent father a wire, but his only response was a terse telegram: 'Return drive chains express mail stop Otherwise car for Munich exhibition cannot move.'

Cars were being made in other countries, notably England and France, but once the Germans had broken the back of the initial notion of making a carriage move without horses it was the French who stepped in to take it from there, initially using the German engines. Ackermann's borrowed idea produced the first tractable 'handling' as we should call it today, and the

Ettore Bugatti's immortal Type 57

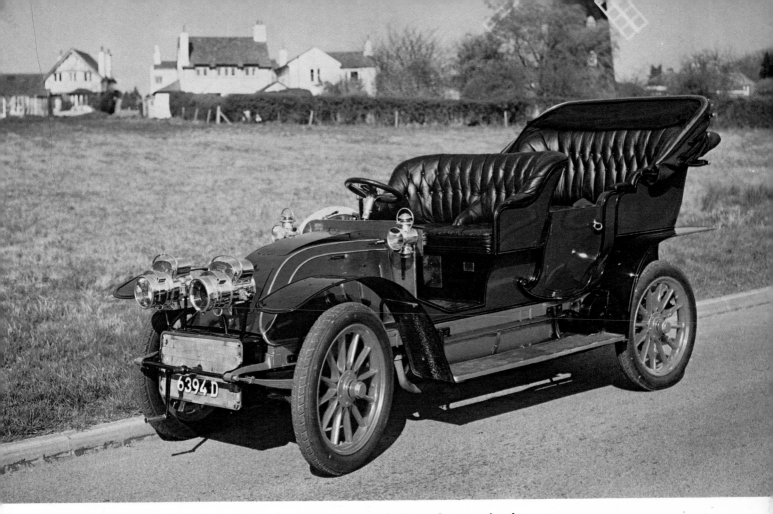

next step was to find a better way of transmitting the engine's power to the wheels than the belts and pulleys which had been borrowed from machine-shop gas-engine practice. This system had offered the first variable gearing by slipping from one size pulley to a larger or smaller one, but was crude and could handle only modest power.

A Frenchman, Emile Levassor, evolved the transmission system of using a friction clutch behind the engine and a gearbox behind that, with an output shaft driving bevel gears to another shaft crosswise from which chains on each side drove both rear

An early French C.G.V. near the windmill at Wray Common, Reigate. If it was English-made it would have been called a Charron after its racing-cyclist maker, whose partners, Girardot and Voigt, were also racing men. Built in 1904, it had a 15 horse-power, four-cylinder engine

The Benz family take a picnic in 1894 with some of the first of their horseless carriages, with *vis-a-vis* (face-to-face) seating

wheels. Curiously E. Lavassor's layout became known by the
name of his partner René Panhard and lives on as the Système
Panhard. This came in 1891, and was later refined by Louis
Renault, who eliminated the chains in favour of a shaft to the
rear axle, which is virtually what we are still using today in
front-engined rear-drive cars.

By 1899 all the great names were showing at the Paris Salon
de l'Automobile: Peugeot, de Dion-Bouton, Panhard, Serpollet,
Mors. By this time the classic pattern of the car as it is still with
us today had emerged. There are still flirtations with steam and
electricity as power sources, but the petrol engine had virtually
taken over and thousands of Benz engines were being used in
cars of his own make and in many others. Some were made in the
Mannheim works and many others either under licence or by
straightforward piracy.

In England the red flag was dispensed with under the 1878 Act,
but the man who formerly carried it still had to walk in front of
the car until 1896, when the mandatory three-man crew provi-
sion was dropped and the permissible speed upped from four
miles an hour to 12. In the United States things were moving
slowly because the large size of the country meant that few
roads had been built, and the roads had to come before the cars.

Morgans do not change much.
Nearer camera is a 1938
model and in background is a
current type being raced today

Looking at the German scene, and seeing all and sundry stealing the Benz design with no profit to the inventor, a Mr H. J. Lawson in England hit on the idea of trying to create a monopoly which would patent and control all automotive production in the country. He had already done very well out of bicycle manufacture, and his first step was to organize a triumphal procession of 30 cars to drive from London to Brighton the day before the November 1896 Act came into force. This was the forerunner of the annual run known by the irreverent as the Old Crocks Race, which is still going strong and now open to cars made before 1904.

Harry John Lawson formed his British Motor Syndicate with capital of £150 000 in 1895. He also formed the Daimler Motor Company and bought the Daimler patents from F. R. Simms, also those of the Count de Dion and many others, but he was unable to enforce his monopoly and eventually after much litigation went into liquidation.

With engines, transmissions and steering which all worked reasonably well within limits, the motorist who now had some measure of reliability began to look for more comfort. The iron-shod wheel or the slightly later solid rubber tyre left something to be desired in this direction, until the pneumatic came upon the scene and transformed the situation. Robert Thompson, who had used solid rubber tyres on his steam carriage, had also made a pneumatic for his horse-drawn carriage as early as 1845, and Dunlop had done the same for the bicycle in 1888. But the first blow-up car tyre did not appear until 1895 when the Michelin brothers fitted them to their entry in the Paris–Bordeaux race. In the 700 miles or so they lost count of the punctures and used up 22 spare tubes.

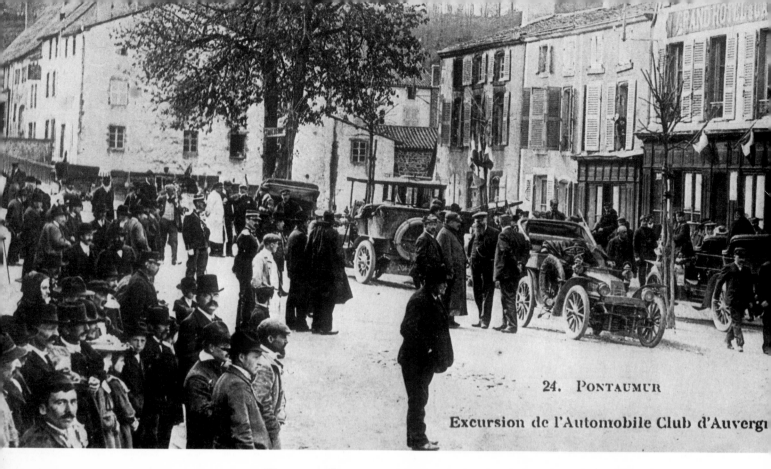

24. PONTAUMUR

Excursion de l'Automobile Club d'Auverg...

above
It could only be France, in fact at Pontaumur, during the Circuit d'Auvergne of the 1905 Gordon Bennett race. Presumably it is some recalcitrant English driver who persists in parking (and driving?) on the left

below
One of many early cars on Benz lines was this twin-cylinder 7 hp Popp, which was built in Basle in 1898

For another ten years motorists fought with the detachable tyre on a non-detachable wheel, which meant that every time they punctured, which was often on the poor roads of the day, they had to force the tyre off the rim with the wheel still in place and change the tube, and probably the cover as well. This usually meant damage to the fingers, and if the tube was nipped by the tyre lever on the way back (a happening familiar to all cyclists) the whole process had to be started all over again. When it was finished there was still to come the hand-pumping of the tyre up to somewhere between 60 and 100 psi.

Tyres made up a big proportion of the cost of motoring, but as technology progressed through the Stepney, a spare rim which could be fixed alongside the existing wheel, to the detachable spare wheel, the durability and resistance to puncturing of the tyre improved too, although right up to the Second World War the puncture was with us. War-time developments led to both the various 'unpuncturable' tyres we have now and to improvements in construction in tyres themselves, particularly when natural rubber was denied to the Western Allies by the Japanese invasion of the Far East.

Once the going was reasonably secure in terms of pace and reliability due to improvements in engines, transmissions, steering, tyres, handling, and other aspects of the horseless carriage the next urgent priority was to be able to stop, and it was a very long time before the instant noiseless halt on demand, on wet or dry roads, was added to the joys of motoring. Early cars followed the horse-carts and carriages with a block of wood or leather to push against the wheel, with a sprag—an iron rod—hanging down underneath ready to be prodded into the ground to halt the backwards escape of the machine if all else failed on a hill.

Then came long-forgotten devices like external-contracting brakes, which were bands attempting to grip a drum within their grasp, and later the drum brake as we know it today in a more refined form. The notion of changing down into a lower gear to

16

use the engine to assist the brakes was not possible on the very early cars because changing was not that easy or instantaneous, and would probably have broken something anyway. But nobody really tried anything except rubbing a piece of friction material against either something attached to the wheels or to the driving shaft. Transmission brakes are still with us, on heavy lorries or coaches in the form of an electrically-operated resistance to turning of the prop-shaft, but the modern brake follows essentially the principle of applying friction to the rotating road wheel to slow it down.

Originally brakes were provided on the back wheels only as it was thought dangerous to attempt to retard the steering wheels at the front as well. Various distinguished people including Sir Henry Royce persisted in this belief for a very long time, and the Rolls-Royce was one of the last makes to adopt four-wheel brakes, as it was to take to the disc. Early examples of four-wheel braking systems were thought to offer such a hazard to the man behind that they carried a warning triangle on the rear of cars so fitted to alert the unwary.

Brakes, like everything else automotive, went through fashions. It was trendy at one time to have finned drums, or aluminium drums, then two-leading shoes and then two-trailing shoes, or self-wrapping shoes and then wire wheels to get more

following pages
An overpoweringly-elegant Rolls-Royce with railway-carriage windows and door-handles shows what we have lost. It is a 40/50 of about 1910 designed to be driven by a hired man who had to put up with the wind and the rain

below
Petrol, electric and steam gather together at the National Motor Museum. The 1901 electric is a Columbia, the Lifu of the same year (on the right) is steam-driven and the petrol-engined car at the back is a De Dietrich

air at the brakes, and scoops for the same reason. Racing and sporty cars of the 1920s offered the driver the facility to make adjustments in the cockpit as he went along. Stretched cables could be taken up with turn-buckles before hydraulics came along to simplify operations.

But brakes are very much the field of the technologist and do not offer much excitement except when they are lacking. Milestones were the adoption of Herbert Frood's discovery that dipping asbestos fibre in a special sauce produced what we now call Ferodo, and the borrowing from aircraft practice of the disc brake. Modern refinements include the pressure-limiting valve to stop the back wheels locking and duplicated circuits for safety, but none of the various magic systems which take the responsibility for a safe stop away from the driver and make it automatic has become cheap enough for universal use. No doubt they will come one day.

There have been curiosities along the way. Many will recall the Austin Seven on which the handbrake worked on the front wheels and the pedal on the rear. There were Frazer-Nashes which effected an economy by having only one rear brake-drum

Miss Speed Festival of 1899 aboard Camille Jenatzy's *Jamais Contente* electric car in which he covered the kilometre at 65.79 mph on a famous stretch of road at Achères

above, left
A Fiat 24/32 of 1903–5
which seems to have suffered
the theft of one headlamp
already. All the early Fiats
were right-hand drive, and to
be pedantic were F.I.A.T.s

above
The Lanchester brothers, Fred
driving and George as
passenger, in one of their 1897
cars, already showing some of
the eccentricities in which
they persisted

as there was no differential in their chain-drive system, so braking one wheel did just as well as braking two. There were systems which did not work very well, but they are best forgotten.

Putting the brakes inboard has been tried, mostly on racing cars, but can lead to costly servicing, which may involve taking the engine out or some major surgery just to reline the brakes. Alvis perpetrated something like this on their front-wheel drive cars. Servo-assistance to lessen the load on the driver's calf-muscles goes back a long way, and has produced systems like the former Rolls-Royce and Bentley one in which the driver has to wait for shafts to wind up cables after he has pressed the pedal before very much happens. Royce originally borrowed the idea of the gearbox-driven servo from Hispano-Suiza and it served well enough before traffic was too thick.

Some comfort came with the air-filled tyre, but when going and stopping and reasonable performance had been achieved people began to want more comfort, which produced changes in suspension systems, not before time, as the cart springs had stayed with the horseless carriage long after the departure of the horses. In fact there are still many cars being made today with a sophisticated version of the cart spring, and they work very well.

It is curious if we look back how many of the ideas regarded as modern were tried in the very early days. In the field of suspension for instance independent springing of the front wheels was tried early on by various people–Lancia and Morgan spring to mind–but not universally adopted until much later in the history of the vehicle. When anyone claims a new idea today its forerunner can usually be dug up back in the mists of time. There was an overhead camshaft in 1901, a supercharger in 1907, electric lighting and starting on Cadillac in the United States by 1912.

Suspension did drag its heels a bit until the Second World War, although by this time the Americans were very inventive and had offered the first independent front-end design on mass-produced cars. They were also using stamped-out one-piece metal bodies, whereas most of Europe was still 'coachbuilding' bodies by nailing pieces of metal on a wooden frame. Exceptions were Citroën and Morris, and others had to follow.

When we had starting, going and stopping taken for granted along with some reliability, drivers became competitive in their attitudes and wanted what we would now call handling and road-holding as well. But the belief persisted right up to the war that the only way to gain the last two was to give away ride comfort, so that a sports car just had to have its springs bound up with

The Morris Eight tourer up to 1938 was the last coachbuilt effort before the company went over to the pressed body seen on its E Type or Series E of 1939

cord and shock absorbers set rock-hard in order to go round corners.

The science of suspension had developed only since the Second World War and owes much to motor racing, where getting the power to the ground and getting round corners as fast as possible is the only route to the championship. Until then there were two breeds of car, the tolerable cheap one in which if that was all you could afford you had to put up with all its deficiencies in ride, handling, roadholding, performance and all other departments, and the costly classic which did everything so much better, including the rapid consumption of fuel.

By this time the split had widened between the European and the American type of car, and the latter with its big engine using cheap fuel offered straight-line performance and comfort at the expense of poor cornering power and braking, whereas the European downmarket machine was noisier, harder-riding but could descend an Alp without losing all its brakes or falling off the side.

To the Americans the motor car was another tool to make life easier, and they developed automatic transmissions, hydraulic brakes, and other devices alongside their independent front-suspension systems, all features aimed at make-it-easy motoring for the masses. In Europe the movement had been more along the lines of the simple and cheap Austin Seven to provide basic transport without frills with a small engine frugal of expensive petrol. Later cars from the big European makers were updated versions of the old recipe revised to suit the times, while the Americans were making their feather-bed monsters bigger and bigger.

Body styles had gone full circle from the first motor car, which began with an open carriage with no weather protection for the occupants and finished up after 50 years with the driver paying more money for a convertible if he wanted to be cold and wet, unless he lived in California. But most travellers had learned that after the first flush of youth open cars are uncomfortable at anything over 50 miles an hour, that wind and noises are tiring. Eventually even the sportsmen discovered that a closed-body shape is more wind-cheating, and now only racing car drivers are regularly exposed to the elements. Safety regulations gave the *coup de grace* to most sports cars or convertibles which were for so long the symbol of wish fulfillment and the attainment of a dream—the last American convertible rolled off the production lines in the spring of 1976.

The classic layout established by Daimler and Benz so long ago is still the dominant in total world production, although front-engine/front-drive has taken over a large slice of the European market. Rear-engine/rear-drive, with which Volkswagen dominated the small-car market for so long, has been superseded. The Mini, which gave the language a new word, also started a revolution in which many others have joined.

In the modern scene the wheel has also turned as petrol, the classic energy source, becomes scarcer and discarded motive powers like steam and electricity are being wooed again after more than half-a-century of neglect. The motor car, once blamed for frightening horses and making unpleasant noises and smells, is again under attack as an anti-social device which causes pollution of the atmosphere and of the environment by its very presence. There is a curious pattern of returning again to what was seen in the beginning, when learned men said man could never survive moving through the air at 60 miles an hour and put as many obstacles as possible in the way of those who wanted to move by motor.

Today the obstacles are coming back, but there are parking meters instead of red flags and now that we can achieve nearly 200 miles an hour, the speed limits in most countries are moving back towards the kind of figures we had in the beginning about 80 years ago. Now that we can have speed and comfort and controlability, safety has become the over-riding consideration, and we must make our cars so that they can bang into each other without too disastrous a result. Daimler and Benz would surely have found it all a little puzzling.

The first two-cylinder Royce of 1904, which was essentially a modified French Decauville. It was very refined for its time, and was produced before Royce met Rolls in Manchester

Motoring comes of Age

When did the motor car become an adult, cease to be a toy and gain the ability status of the bed, the refrigerator, the daily newspaper? One of the biggest milestones in the history of the motor car was the arrival of the Model T Ford, as this had one of the longest production runs and biggest outputs of all cars. As it was also undeniably a tool of the trade of millions of people it must rank as a useable daily tool and not in any way a toy or passing fancy. More than 15 million were made in a 19-year run. The first one appeared in 1908.

This seems a very early year to set as the date that the car had made it, survived its teething and other infant troubles; on the basis that the car had moved from the realm of amusement to that of the workhorse, however, it must stand up to all tests. Perhaps one way to make an assessment is to look at the humour of the motor car as expressed in cartoons and note at what stage it has ceased to be regarded as an eccentricity and been accepted as part of the scenery of everyday life. The early jokes were concerned with funny clothing, speed traps, tyre troubles and breakdowns and these topics went on into the 1920s, although by then we had closed coachwork (no funny clothes) and reasonable reliability.

The year 1908 does seem a precocious time to choose on the basis of the public's attitude as reflected in the cartoons, but we can hardly ignore the Model T, and a workhorse it undoubtedly was. Yet at that time learned people were still writing articles on 'How to dress for motoring' and similar topics, and treated the car as a special sort of device which had to be chosen with care, and in which one wore peculiar clothes. It had also to be kept in a specially-built 'motor house', needed its own attendant, and was the object of various strange rituals. A doctor advocated running for 200 or 300 yards at the end of a 20-mile motor drive, but said he thought it was a healthy occupation just as good for the liver as horse riding.

These attitudes are deduced from English publications of the time which tended to be written by noble lords and ladies. Yet our friend the Model T must have stood in farmyards or open-sided barns in many cases and certainly had few rituals performed around it. Was there a big gulf between European and American attitudes and usage? That may be the explanation, as for example the Sunday whirring of dusters as the family car is cleaned has always been a British rather than an American sound, and the different national attitudes may go almost back to the beginning.

right
The kind of motoring with funny clothes which made a cartoonist's holiday. These three White Steamers successfully completed an endurance run of 100 miles on Long Island, New York, in April 1902

below
Street scene USA needs only Laurel and Hardy to complete the picture. All the cars are Model Ts and the road is unsealed. The cranking chauffeur is dressed for protection against the rising dust

right
Model T Fords, about 1913, coming off the line at the Highland plant. Bodies are coming down the slope to drop onto the chassis below, a method not so different from that used today

By 1908 many long-distance demonstrations or trials had been staged, and there was not much doubt that a car could cover 1 000 miles or so with minimal service or breakdown, although cars produced by their manufacturers for special demonstrations may not always be absolutely typical ones taken off the production line! There were also by this time Grand Prix cars, which although hardly representative of the average commercial traveller's transport were capable of more than 100 miles an hour, which is a respectable rate, even if illegal in some parts of the world, 70 years later.

The Silver Ghost was also with us although it had not yet demonstrated its reliability in the famous London–Edinburgh run to counter S. F. Edge's effort with the Napier. But even earlier, in 1905, a Napier ran from Brighton to Edinburgh without changing gear. All these cars and their efforts may seem remote from the workaday Model T, but we are trying to offer some comparison with the state of the art in Europe compared with that in the USA, where they had started motoring later but perhaps progressed more quickly. In our datum year of 1908 Cadillacs had put on a startling demonstration in England when seven of their cars were assembled from mixed kits of parts, and then driven round a circuit to prove the interchangeability of their components. This was an eye-opener in an age of hand-made pieces which could rarely be swapped from one car to another.

But our grown-up car of 1908, if we are going to stick by that date, would not have offered us the home comforts we all expect nowadays. It would not have had for instance a self-starter. Such devices had been fitted to a few cars but were not in general use. The electric horn also existed but we were more likely to be given a Klaxon which made that lovely raucous noise of metal scraping over metal but was very much manually operated, with the palm of the hand on the big button.

A superb, Cunard-bodied Napier 30/35 of 1913. This company was a rival of Rolls-Royce, and later was pre-empted by Rolls-Royce in an attempt to buy the failed Bentley company

The first Chevrolet produced in 1912 has electric lights, Klaxon, pneumatic tyres, windscreen, hood and a much later look about it, although only 2 999 came out of the Detroit works that year. In the next 50 years the company notched up 45 million

Nor would we have had the facility of instant electric lighting at the touch of a switch. C. A. Vandervell, later famous both in the electrical manufacture and racing car field, were pioneers of such lighting sets, but batteries had to be taken from the car for charging. There was no way of restoring their life *in situ*, although expert amateurs were playing with charge-it-yourself dynamos screwed onto their cars. On the other hand, the acetylene lamp was at the crest of its development and offered adequate illumination, not instantaneously at the touch of a switch but after a little ceremony with carbide and water.

Many European cars were still driven by chains, although M. Renault's development of shaft drive to the rear axle was becoming more popular. Ignition systems had improved, the hot tube and low-tension systems had gone, although our Model T would still have used a simple trembler-coil. We would also have been limited to rear-wheel brakes and an absence of weather-protection except a hood, but the car cost only 850 dollars.

Perhaps in spite of the undoubted practicality of the Model T we should in all honesty shift our sights a little higher and demand electric starting and lighting, four-wheel braking, saloon bodywork, and some other modern comforts—but where to end? Do we insist on heating, windscreen wipers and such luxuries? The difficulty about making such demands is that there is no universal date on which all countries complied, and we would need a league table of who fits what to reach any conclusion.

The two world wars have provided convenient dates for measuring many human activities, and played a big part in the development of the motor car from its intensive military use, although it was denied to most civilians at the same time. So if we advance six years to 1914 how does the picture change, and does it make a fairer choice? It so happens that this particular slice of automotive history has been called 'the years of refinement', so it may bring us some worthwhile rewards.

Front-wheel brakes began to appear from about 1910 onwards, so we might have been lucky by 1914 if we chose the right make.

Up to this time some makers were still using materials like leather or wood for their mud-wings, a hangover from the carriage days, but we might expect metal ones by the start of the war. The pressed-steel wheel in place of the spoked-wire wheel or the wooden wheel had been introduced and was cheaper to make, easier to maintain, and easier to clean.

Electricity was pushing its way in for lighting and starting – Cadillac had offered both as standard fittings in 1912 – but compressed air was still very much in vogue for commencing the bigger engines, which were tiresome to swing for those who did not employ A Man for the purpose (and also to drive and clean the car). In England there were 265 000 vehicles registered, 132 000 of them cars, which is four times as many as on our earlier chosen date. We might also have expected to have been provided with a spare wheel by 1914.

Reverting to Our Man for a moment, Lord Northcliffe wrote at the time, 'A prime difficulty of the establishment of a motor car is the chauffeur or engineer. The perfect motor servant should be a combination of gentleman and engineer. He is a new type of man, and will require the wages of other engineers. I do not think that a competent, cool-headed, skilful, well-mannered head engineer will ever be obtainable for 30 shillings a week.'

above
The first Royce posed in 1924, twenty years after it was built, with a 40/50 outside the Cooke St, Manchester works where it was made. The 40/50 may have lights and weather protection but it still lacks front wheel brakes

left
Red Square in Moscow before the revolution. The cars are Laurin and Klement Type FC, made from 1908 to 1913, which is as closely as it can be pin-pointed in time, but they look like racers with their twin spare wheels and bolster tanks

Some of the forgotten hazards of those early days include the theft of lamps when a car was left parked, and one accessory firm featured 'prickly' wing nuts to hold on the lamps which would hurt the would-be thief's fingers. By this time some car makers were mixing their lamps, using electricity for the sidelamps and acetylene for the headlamps, which in some cases were claimed to produce 10 000 candle-power.

Sporting activities were much closer to the general motor user than they are today. Road racing was well-established in Europe and had enjoyed a brief flowering in the USA, the Brooklands track was in full use and at Indianapolis the '500' was on its way to becoming an institution, and long-distance trials which were the forerunners of rallies were proving the virtues and finding the weaknesses of touring cars. Cars were being developed in competition on both sides of the Atlantic. With the various developments which had succeeded each other, over the years raising the general level of performance in the wider sense, running costs had also fallen, and just before the 1914 war it was said that a small car could be run in England for five pence a mile, which was half the cost of a pony and trap.

Results of the off-track races and trials, hill-climbs and other competitions had a big effect upon the sales of the different makes of car and even Rolls-Royce were pitting their wares against the Continentals in European trials in France, Austria and Germany. Nothing seems to have changed much, as shrewd dealers were making money by buying heavy saloons, tuning the engines and fitting light sporting bodies to suit the young men of the day.

A new light car which a more everyday type of motorist would choose cost about £250 in the immediate pre-war days, and some people quoted costs even lower than the fivepence a mile already mentioned. Big cars were of course an entirely different proposition and appealed to a different type of owner who could keep A Man to deal with all the servicing and other problems. But the changing world was moving towards a vehicle which the ordinary driver could afford to buy and maintain himself without paid assistance, and the 1914–18 war dealt the final blow to the car which needed a chauffeur, except for production in small numbers for the few people who could afford it. The accent was on making cars which were cheap to manufacture and cheap to run.

The First World War had an enormous effect on the development of the automobile. Production stopped in England, France

Steam came and went, sadly
leaving us with all that
polluted air. This Stanley
Runabout of 1910 shows that
steam cars did not look very
different from a petrol car,
and they were a lot quieter

left
The American Underslung of
1915 seems dwarfed by its
artillery wheels with detachable
Stepney rims. Note the
buttoned upholstery, Cape
cart-type hood and, already,
electric lights

and Germany except for military purposes, but as the United
States was not involved until several years later output of civilian vehicles continued and developed. They were behind Europe
in some technical aspects when the war began, but ahead in
others, perhaps mainly related to methods of production in
which they have remained world leaders.

But what about our date for the coming of age party? We must
ignore the war years when design was at a standstill throughout
Europe even where some production continued, which means
effectively jumping to about 1919–20 to find resumed production,
although of the same cars which we had known and possibly
loved before the conflict. Some people think of the 'twenties as
the golden age of motoring, but it was only golden for the few
until vehicles like the Austin Seven and Citroën 5CV–if there
are or could be any other vehicles like an Austin Seven or a
Cloverleaf Citroën–were made in large numbers for the family
man who could afford to move up-market from the motor-cycle
combination.

In European terms it would be reasonable to take the Austin
and the Citroën as equivalents of the Model T Ford in that they
brought the practical motor car to the man in the street, and if
we equate the differences in national incomes and the cost of fuel
they fulfilled the same function–offering cheap basic transport
with low initial cost and easy, cheap servicing. In the Model T,
Ford cheated a little by adding electric lights and horn in 1914,
although these were worked from the flywheel magneto and
could thus cause kangaroo petrol effects if used with the engine
running slowly, by stealing much-needed volts from the engine
coils. Full electrical equipment including starting and the

dynamo did not come until 1919. This overcame the problem of all T owners of being in danger of being run over by their own car every time they used the starting handle, as the epicyclic transmission had built-in creep, just like the modern automatic transmission, and was liable to pin its fond owner to the barn door. Nowadays makers of two-pedal units boast about the built-in creep as a manoeuvring advantage, whereas the truth of the matter is that they cannot get rid of it.

Now our Baby Austin came on the scene in 1922 but did not acquire electric starting until 1924, which puts our coming-of-age back a bit if we are going to insist on all mod cons as part of the deal. True, some early Babies had a hand-starter inside the car which could turn the engine one-and-a-half times, but this hardly counts as the real thing.

The more one thinks about it the more valid the comparison between these two so-different cars becomes as harbingers of motoring for all in their respective countries. By the start of the war the Model T was selling in England for £135, and although the Seven cost £225 when it came on the market it was down to £165 by the end of the same year (1922). The T was a lot more car for the money, had much more ground clearance, and could carry more people or things. But someone once said when asked if the Americans had a higher standard of living than Europeans: 'They have more things,' which is not necessarily a positive answer.

These cars had a maximum speed of 45–50 miles an hour, whatever boastful owners may say, although the Ford had a 2·9-litre engine against the Austin's pitiful 747 cc and the Citroën's 856 cc. Acceleration was best measured with an egg-timer, as you

Indianapolis followed relatively hot on the heels of Britain's Brooklands. This photograph shows the grid for the first '500' in 1911. The Stoddart-Dayton pace car on the right is being cranked to start, front row cars (left to right) are a Case, a Simplex, an Interstate and a National

33

Herbert Austin's Seven came with a world fit for heroes to live in after the First World War, in 1922 when the ex-soldier wanted cheap transport, and has become a cult today in spite of its crudities

could have a one-minute egg in the time it took to reach 50 miles an hour. We could pursue the comparison ad nauseum, but the point has been made. The Ford and the Austin acquired a variety of body styles, in the case of the Austin not always from the works but conceived by outside coachbuilders with varying ideas of absurdity. Some of them were very good cars for very small people, but offered problems for a six-foot man who also had a head. The T did not suffer in this way. The Austin would go at least twice as far on a gallon of fuel, but this is not really relevant as petrol was then so cheap on the T's home ground.

By today's standards these cars suffered from many deficiencies, and it begins to look as if we will have to put off the birthday party even further into the century to accommodate all the attributes which we now demand as original equipment on even the cheapest motor car.

When it comes down to controlability or handling neither of these two could score very high marks at the sort of speeds which are now considered normal, although they were adequate within the frame of their own capabilities, as an advertising man might say. When it comes to a question of stopping, perhaps the less said the better.

But there is about the cars of the 1920s, both in the flesh or metal and in contemporaneous photographs and films, some kind of attraction which is difficult to define. When one comes to drive them they may be disappointing, but the wealth of wood and leather on the more costly models, the satisfying clunky shut of the doors, the elaborate castings and careful finishing of details, adds up to a finished product which gives pleasure to look at. Our modern machines may go faster and use less fuel, and be more reliable, but they can rarely satisfy the pride of ownership concept which the old car fulfills, which is the reason for the great nostalgia industry which has grown up around the Edwardian, Veteran, Vintage and so on cars, more simply grouped as 'Classics' in the US.

But such considerations are really outside our brief in fixing the date of the birthday party. We are concerned with practicalities rather than aesthetics or undefinable virtues which may make us fall in love with some vehicle which is absolutely ghastly by any reasonable standard. So what must we have?

above
What the sporting young man coveted in 1911, the Prince Henry Vauxhall designed by Laurence Pomeroy senior

left
Ettore Bugatti in one of his early cars, which is not too well equipped for luggage carrying, an idea which came later to most manufacturers and much later for Bugatti drivers, who were said to tape their toothbrush to the outside handbrake

The specification so far takes in what now seem such obvious necessities as four-wheel brakes, pneumatic tyres, electric lighting and starting, closed coachwork if desired, reliability. What must be added to complete the transformation not from pumpkin to carriage but from perhaps a craftsman's joy to a commercial traveller's friend and ally?

We are now in the 1920s and any one old enough will recall that starting a car on a cold morning was not always the automatic process it is today. But the routine of taking out and warming plugs, pouring hot water on vital parts, tickling carburetters to flood them, stuffing rags into air intakes, pushing and/or towing, went on to a much later date than this. The magneto, which was something of a villain of the piece, must take its share of blame. It had a reputation for producing a better spark, and was often chosen by those who wanted high performance for racing or maybe just for fast road driving in preference to the humble coil, as it was – and still is – said to be reliable up to a higher rate of engine revolutions.

This may be valid for racing purposes, but one suspects that on road cars it fell into the same category as stoneguards for the lamps of cars which never left the tarmac, although their alleged object was not cosmetic but to protect the glasses from stones thrown up on Alpine dirt roads. Many other fittings and accessories of the period fell into this category, and we saw little sports cars which could hardly drag themselves along festooned with twin spare wheels, Le Mans slab tanks, stoneguards, giant spot lights, and all sorts of fripperies. It did brighten the scene to gaze upon such a variety of body styles and added decoration, but how much of the extra equipment had any real function is another matter.

But to return to our sparks and our old friend or enemy the magneto. This device did perhaps function for longer periods without attention than the coil and distributor system which succeeded it, but it was much more of a mystery to the amateur mechanic. Certainly if it became old and tired it was reluctant to push out the energy it should. It was also more expensive to manufacture, which maybe had as much to do with its demise for bread and butter use as the simpler reliability of coil ignition.

In this period–the 1920s–some manufacturers of expensive cars hedged their bets or wore both belt and braces by offering dual ignition with both coil and magneto. Rolls-Royce were one, but in their case it was not a simple dashboard switchover but entailed opening the bonnet and pulling out a lead and replacing one end in a different hole. They also used a lower-voltage coil– about nine volts on a 12-volt system–with a booster spark, an arrangement which has come back again on some current mass-produced cars.

So are we agreed that we must postpone the birthday again to take in the advent of the instant spark of the coil? For bear in mind that the marvellous magneto with all its high-performance adjuncts had to be whizzed round some before it would perform its allotted task with any enthusiasm. Sparking plugs themselves do not appear to have changed much in design over the years, but they have undoubtedly been improved in efficiency, and with coil ignition it is less critical to fumble a start if the gaps are too wide than with the tired magneto.

Coil ignition belongs to the 1930s, which is pushing us along again towards the Second World War. What else helped over-come our early morning sickness in regard to starting apart from a better source of spark? Improved carburation and better mani-folding might be named, and the use of lighter oils, or oils with less drag to impose heavy loads on the starter. Dates? Impossible to limit it to any one year, as continued development led on step by step towards a more assured departure time in the morning. Improved battery techniques helped also. Perhaps the date when starting handles began to disappear would give us a clue that it had been proved, to the manufacturers' satisfaction at least, that we did not need them any more. This was a development of the late 1940s, which led to a lot of acrimony from those of the old school who like to 'ease the pain' of their batteries by a few turns on the handle before the starter was used. That idea seems to have disappeared along with the old practice of letting the engine warm up for a few minutes before driving off, which is now condemned as causing more wear than it avoids.

What else is there which is relevant to our date-search which aided easy starting? Fuel technology no doubt, although im-mediately after the Second World War many Europeans were still condemned for a long time to poor petrol, equivalent in octane rating to the lowest commercial grade today.

It is a long time since the driver in the party would say before a journey: 'I'll just go and see if she will start', but only subjec-tive memory can date that one. Modern owners of vintage cars

above
Sportsman's carriage of the
1912 era, a Hispano-Suiza
Alfonso, built for the young
Spanish king and sold in
chassis form for only £400.
They were said to do 70 mph
(without front brakes) and
returned more than 20 mpg

left
The rugged early days with
nothing between you and the
elements. Car is an Apperson
Jack Rabbit, built from 1907
to sell at 5 000 dollars 'for
racing or touring', and with a
guaranteed 75 miles-an-hour
speed

will insist that their cars always did start first go on the button, but they forget that they now use modern batteries, fuels, plugs and who knows what else.

So must we really shift forward again to after the Second World War to find our every-morning start? This can be argued until the battery runs flat, but it seems a fair assumption. Then how about the ancillary frills like heating and ventilation, in-car entertainment as radio seems to be called, signalling of our intention to turn or stop, and the many safety devices like seat belts and crash padding which we now take for granted?

Working backwards we must eliminate the safety aids as not essential to motoring, however desirable they might be, and so rule them out of our required specification. The same goes for radio, although if we do want to be difficult about this one there have been car radio sets of a sort for a very long time, and some people find they do not work terribly well even today. Picnic scenes of the 1920s show the portable set in use on the running board, although it was a massive and heavy device.

Turning and stopping indicators have also been around for a very long time, although hardly essential requisites to driving. Hand signals went out a very long time ago and the brake light has been with us since before the Second World War, and there were some amusing attempts at direction indicators. Talbots had winking arrows under the radiator and in a box on the back of the car, and Morris offered a miniature set of traffic lights showing green for go, yellow for slowing down and red for stopping, but this was ruled illegal in England. Before this there were plastic hands worked by cable, which must have frightened susceptible people behind when they materialised without benefit of arm over the side of an open car.

Heating and ventilation offers ground for dispute too. First we had the car which was air-conditioned by being completely open, then came the windscreen, the rag roof, the sidescreens. When bodies became closed, the little trapdoor in the roof let out the old air and windows slid up and down on railway carriage straps until the winder appeared, to let in the new air, although some of that would have already found its own way in through gaps and cracks in the days before dust-sealing rubbers were thought of.

Then came the sunroof or the convertible, and now we have gone full circle and shut out all the fresh air and can even manufacture our own if we spend enough money. This aspect too, we can leave out of account in our dating exercise as we can still motor up to a point even if our tiny hands are frozen and our neck aching from the draught.

Many aspects we still have not tackled. How about luggage? Must we have under-cover accommodation? A famous driver of a Bugatti Type 35, which takes one-and-a-half people and nothing else, solved the week-end luggage problem by taping his toothbrush to the outside handbrake, but perhaps that was cheating. The lovely old tailored trunks on the outside grid have long gone, and the boot swallows all. But this had been done by the time the war came, although there were cars—even big-production models like some Morrises—which offered only a space behind the rear seat and no way of reaching it except by hauling the suitcases in through the side doors and over the front seats, then under the raised back-seat rest into the hole. And this was as late as 1937, when most of the masochism had gone out of motoring, except as an optional extra in open sports cars.

Just as nobody has reached a better definition of a sports car than the one which said it was a vehicle which one could not walk through wearing a top hat, so we are not much closer arranging the date of the coming-of-age party for the motor car, but it is an enjoyable exercise to speculate and recall the delightful eccentricities of designers over the years. A favourite mirth-provoker was the Startix, which was supposed to aid lady drivers and persisted in trying to start an engine which had stalled, sometimes after the driver had gone away, and went on until the car ran out of either petrol or battery. No doubt the man's intentions were good.

Definition of spartan: an early Morgan like this one, without mudguards, windscreens or any concession to the elements— but with independent front suspension and a happy driver

The Sportsmen

The first true motor race, the 732-mile Paris-Bordeaux-Paris, came in 1895 when the motor car was only ten years old. Here is the winner, Emile Levassor, on his Panhard, the oldest make of all.

opposite, top
Louis Renault, driving one of his own cars with the coal-skuttle bonnet, is told of the death of his brother Marcel in the infamous Paris-Madrid of 1903, which was stopped at Bordeaux as there were so many casualties

opposite, lower
Riding mechanic ready to leap out and change a wheel—or more accurately a rim—in one of the first Grand Prix races on roads which caused frequent punctures

The motor car was born but hardly toddling in November 1894, when sportsmen gathered together to see whose car could go fastest. The meeting was on November 18 at the home of the Count de Dion, one of France's pioneer manufacturers, and those present planned a great race from Paris to Bordeaux and back, a distance of 732 miles, to be made in one trip. The contestants were allowed to make repairs only with such spares and tools as could be carried on the machine, a rule which later applied to such great events as the Le Mans 24-hour race. They were allowed to procure on route nothing but 'entertainment for man and machine', which is a curious choice of phrase, presumably translated from the French and losing its meaning on the way.

The rollcall of those at the meeting includes many names which became household words in motoring circles: Baron de Zuylen, the Count de Dion (of course), the Marquis de Chasseloup-Laubat, the Count de Chasseloup-Laubat, P. Gauthier, Ravenez, Peugeot, Levassor, Serpollet, Dufayel, Lavellette, Recoppe, Roger, Menier, de Place, Giffard, Émile Gauthier, Meillan, Nansouty and Moreau. This list is quoted from an article by the Marquis de Chasseloup-Laubat, and it is typical of the arrogant attitude of the nobleman that the commoners do not even have their christian names listed except when it is necessary in order to tell one from the other, as in the case of the two Gauthiers.

The Marquis was a founder-member of the Automobile Club de France, and his brother Count Gaston was the first man to hold the world land speed record. Purists will say that there is no such thing, but the fastest speed over the flying kilometre or mile has been so titled since 1898 when Count Gaston set it at 39·24 mph with his electric Jeantaud car. He held the record three times in all over the years, but ran in one direction only over the kilometre, as the later rule requiring a two-way run in opposite directions had not yet been made.

Of those present Léon Serpollet also took the world record in 1902 with his steam car at 75·06 mph. Contemporary critics said his car looked like a boat turned upside down. Of the others de Dion, Peugeot, Levassor, and Serpollet all became motor manufacturers, and others played their roles as racing drivers. The race was planned for June 1895, and was the second motoring competition; the very first event was run from Paris to Rouen in 1894, and was not a race, although it had some of the elements of a race. A de Dion-Bouton steam carriage made the fastest time—

almost 12 mph – but because the vehicle was in effect a tractor and trailer, the first prize was awarded jointly to a Panhard and a Peugeot.

It is worthwhile taking a brief look at the preparations for the Paris–Bordeaux race as it set the pattern for so much of what was to follow in motor racing for many years to come, rightly or wrongly. The French never suffered from the English problem of a ban on racing on public roads and they co-opted onto their race committee people like the government official in charge of roads and bridges and the local Deputies or Members of Parliament. They also had two Americans, Gordon Bennett and W. K. Vanderbilt, who were soon sponsoring their own races.

The French committee obviously knew all about public relations, even if the term had not then been invented, as they had all the contesting cars on parade in a public exhibition for several days before the event, 'which attracted much notice'. Emile Levassor, who collaborated with René Panhard as a manufacturer, covered the course in 48 hours 48 minutes running time more or less non-stop, averaging 15 mph. His car, of his own make, used a Daimler engine and did not have a single breakdown. Once again, the fastest driver and vehicle did not win, for Levassor's car was a two-seater and as the regulations specified that the first four-seat car to finish would win, Koechlin in a Peugeot took the main award.

Fifteen petrol and six steam cars started this race, but eight petrol and only one steamer finished, which the Marquis called the triumph of petrol over steam. There was only one electric car, which failed to finish. Thus began the fashion for town-to-town races, Paris–Marseilles, Paris–Vienna and so on, which came to a sticky end with the infamous Paris–Madrid of 1903 when there were so many accidents that the race was stopped at Bordeaux and the cars impounded by the police and dragged to the station yard by horses.

Gabriel on a Mors won, although he had started number 168, and covered the 342 miles at 65·3 mph. But it was the end of the great town-to-town races, although racing sometimes under the name of 'trials' continued on public roads in Continental Europe, and also on closed circuits with normal traffic banned, as in the Circuit des Ardennes run over a 53·5-mile lap. The Gordon Bennett Trophy series, backed by the American newspaper better known for sending Stanley to look for Livingstone, were first run with the town-to-town epics, and then succeeded them. The Gordon Bennett races were open to teams of three from each country, nominated by its chief motoring club, and this arrangement led to a great deal of acrimony, especially as France, the leading motoring nation, felt that this type of equality was not fair.

They were a milestone in the history of motor sport, as previous events had been fought out by the cars offered for sale to the public, but now people began building 'racers' for the first time, and if they could also sell them afterwards, well, so much the

Mercedes 60 in full cry. This is a preserved 1904 example of the classic model which won the 1903 Gordon Bennett race

better. The classic instance is the Mercedes 60 and 90 which swept all before them.

Every history book relates how Mercedes set the fashion for all cars in 1901 by introducing the pressed-steel chassis, honeycomb radiator and gate gear-change, which together with the mechanically-operated inlet valve were copied by all others including Fiat, the American Locomobile, the French Peugeot and the British Star. But the amusing thing about the racing situation was that Mercedes planned to run a team of their 11·9-litre 90s in the Gordon Bennett in 1903, which was to be run in Ireland as such things could not be done in England, and it was England's turn to be host as they had won the year before in France.

But on the eve of the race the team cars were destroyed by fire at Cannstatt, so they had to borrow some 60s back to run in their place and succeeded in winning with the red-bearded Camille Jenatzy at the wheel. This is all rather by-the-way to the important point that it was Mercedes who pointed the way to build special racing cars with a view to winning under a particular set of rules, a notion which was very much taken to by all the racing-car constructors from then on.

Motor racing in the heroic age was in many ways much more gripping than it has been ever since, when very brave drivers with their even braver mechanics sitting or crouching beside them roared through the dust on dirt roads with little visibility, on tyres which burst frequently, with chains thrashing under their elbow, and no brakes to speak of. Many of the drivers were

The mettlesome monster had its fiery day in racing, although this 1911 Delage *Coupe de l'Auto* from France is one of the less extreme examples of the breed. The modern day owner, seen aboard, is Sir John Briscoe

End of the 'age of monsters' in Grand Prix racing came when Georges Boillot won the 1912 French GP in this Peugeot. Car had a fast-revving twin-ohc 7.6-litre engine, and was proved superior to rivals with engines twice the size. Boillot supervises a refuelling stop, with mechanics working from a trench—this gave the word 'pit' to the English racing language

opposite, top
Wagner's Mercedes, one of the triumphant German team, at the pits during the 1914 French Grand Prix

opposite, lower
Camille Jenatzy at the winning post after victory in the 1903 Gordon Bennet Cup on the Mercedes 60, which showed how a high-performance car should be built

car manufacturers, others were paid to do the job, and there was something of the aura of the gladiator about the leather-clad figures who set out on a long-distance race with little idea what disasters lay ahead. If they finished without a mechanical explosion of some kind or an almighty excursion off the road it was an occasion, and if they won, well that was a bonus.

Words cannot portray the spectacle of the giant racers sliding on the loose surface at speeds which would frighten many of us today, and the same drivers in the same cars did hill climbs, grand prix races, speed trials or whatever competition turned up. Specialization came later, the first division being at the turn of the century, when in 1901 cars were split into four classes according to weight.

Thus began the idea of trying to set out some equality of competition, which was later tried according to engine size as is done today. Other methods tried were by limiting fuel consumption or specifying particular fuels, but always clever entrants found ways to cheat legally, or sometimes not quite so legally, which led ultimately to the scrutineering which we have today before races, and the stripping and examining of engines afterwards.

In 1906 the French organized the first Grand Prix, run over 769 miles at Le Mans and won by Ferenc Szisz in a Renault. In the following years the French were mortified to see 'their' race, the premier race, fall to Fiat and Mercedes. There were to be occasional lapses, but the idea of Grand Prix racing was established, and although other national Grands Prix were not to be run until after the First World War the roots of today's world championship series had taken hold.

The heroic age ended about 1908 when the giant machines of 12 and 13 litres gave place to engines which dwindled in size down to an ultimate 1·5 litres by 1926, when what had been called voiturettes or light cars became the main contestants. Yet the 1·5-litre Delage of 1927 showed a top speed of 128 mph against the 1908 12-litre Fiat's 100 mph, proving that either time or racing had improved the breed.

U 104

Stirling Moss found it too hot in the Lotus at Monaco in 1961, so had the side-panels of Rob Walker's car removed and the fans could see the organist at work on the pedals

The 1920s was another great decade in the annals of racing, when the 'characters' among drivers were as thick as starlings at twilight. There are more legends about Tazio Nuvolari than most, about how he drove in plaster over broken bones from a previous accident, and another time was lifted onto his motor cycle swathed in bandages to win a race in pouring rain. He did not start racing until he was nearly 30, yet notched up nearly 50 major wins, driving in his last race when 58 years old. He wore a leather waistcoat over a high-necked yellow pullover, blue trousers with white tennis shoes, and a leather helmet, pulled funny faces, waved his arms about and generally gave the crowd a wonderful show. Brakes did not interest him much, and there is a story that he drove the 1934 Italian Grand Prix virtually without any, as the mechanics had drained the fluid to lose weight for the weigh-in.

He is credited with inventing the four-wheel drift, and certainly drove in a style which nobody else had matched, sliding the car into corners at apparently impossible speeds. Tazio had much sadness in his private life; both his sons died before they were 20. Yet he was always the laughing cavalier in action, until the illness which eventually killed him in 1953 when he was 61 began to take its toll. One of the effects was an allergy to petrol or carbon monoxide fumes, and for a man who was always around motor cars this made life very difficult, and he eventually wore a mask over his nose and mouth.

Nobody could match Tazio's record or personality, but there were many other colourful figures from the same era, among them Giuseppe Campari, Louis Chiron, Achille Varzi, Hans Stuck, the mercurial Berndt Rosemeyer and Rudolf Caracciola, best remembered for his superb skill in the wet. His successor in this regard was Stirling Moss, who was always said to like driving in the rain, but eventually admitted after his retirement that he hated it just as much as anyone else but it was good psychological warfare to let the other drivers think he was happy before the start.

Caracciola was German, born 1901, and he spent most of his driving life with Mercedes until his death in 1959. With the vast 7-litre sports cars of the early 1930s he won his title of Regenmeister (Rainmaster) and was in action from 1922 to 1952, when he was so badly injured in practice for a sports car race at Berne that he never drove again. He won sports car races, grand prix races and hill-climbs with equal ability, and is perhaps best remembered for his unmatched six victories in the German Grand Prix—all save one of them at the demanding Nürburgring—his Mille Miglia victory in 1931, and his supreme drive through foul weather to win the 1929 Ulster Grand Prix.

Caracciola was seriously injured several times in his career, and was out of racing for years at a time due to broken bones and complications afterwards. He lived in Switzerland during the war when he was out of sympathy with the Nazi government of Germany.

above, left
Some say the greatest driver
ever, Tazio Nuvolari, in his
Alfa in the 1931 Mille Miglia,
the 1 000-mile town-to-town
race which was the last such
event to survive

above
Fangio, the Grand Prix master,
in action in a Maserati 250F
during the 1957 French GP.
He won the world championship five times. The 250F
stands alone amongst racing
cars of the period

It is difficult to pick out the great or the most interesting of the
men of speed throughout the more than 80 years that motor
racing has been going on since that decisive Paris meeting in
1894, and a complete directory of all the thousands of drivers
would be too long and boring, so the best we can do is to pull out
a plum here and there down the years from all the personalities
who have had so many stories and legends built up around them.

As the threads of racing were picked up again after the
Second World War, most of the cars had their origins in the
1930s–the Alfa Romeo 158 which had been raced in 1938–39 was
to be developed to dominate Grand Prix racing until 1951–and
the star drivers were of the older generation. But Louis Chiron,
stylish Giuseppe Farina, who was to become the first world

champion in 1949, Jean-Pierre Wimille and others were soon to
be challenged and surpassed by newcomers, such as Alberto
Ascari and above all the Argentinian Juan Manuel Fangio. He
was to drive Alfa Romeo, Mercedes-Benz, Ferrari and Maserati
cars to five world championships—a record that has never been
equalled. Even while Fangio was at the height of his power,
however, a new type of professional racing driver was emerging.

Stirling Moss, already briefly mentioned, was of that new
generation and although never world champion his is one of the
names which are known throughout the world even to people
who take no interest in motor sport. Perhaps this is because he
was successful when he was very young, and was also the first of
the post-war generation of drivers to make a great deal of money
from the sport and let people know about it. Or it may be just
that he was at the crest of the wave when public interest turned
the spotlight on motor sport, which had before been something
of a private world in which few people took any interest, certainly in England.

This all changed when an old aerodrome, Silverstone, was
taken over by the British Racing Drivers Club after the Second
World War and the sort of crowd hitherto seen only at a cup
final turned out to see a race, aroused by the publicity provided
by the *Daily Express*, which had taken the sport under its wing
as a circulation builder. Moss came along at just the right time,
and proved to have a natural talent allied to the right connec-
tions—a racing mother and father—and shot to the top, although
not always a good picker when it came to choosing his mount.

above
Alberto Ascari, famous son of a
famous father, in the big
$4\frac{1}{2}$- litre Ferrari on the way to
win at San Remo in 1951

right
Dentist Tony Brooks winning
the 1955 Syracuse Grand Prix
in his Connaught, first
British driver in a British car
to win a GP for more than
20 years

below
Juan Manuel Fangio using
the Mercedes air brake on the
Sarthe circuit in the Le Mans
24-hour race in 1955, year of
the greatest disaster in racing
history

Moss was born in 1929 and began racing at 18 in Formula 3, which was for motor-cycle engined miniature cars intended to be the poor man's motor racing formula, but soon became very expensive when people began using works racing motor-cycle engines which they obtained by buying a complete machine and using only the engine. He was an immediate success and British champion at 20, then went on to win Coupes des Alpes in the Alpine Rally, a road event for sports cars and an entirely different province from circuit racing, although more akin to road racing than the type of rough-road rally which is run today.

Moss originally determined to drive British and turned down a rare offer from Ferrari, but later was with both Mercedes and Maserati. He was runner-up for the world championship in three successive years and one other (1956–58 and 1961) but never claimed the top spot. When teamed up with the great Argentinian Juan Manuel Fangio, for Mercedes, Moss the young Englishman and Fangio old enough to be his father made one of the great teams of all time.

Moss drove many different kinds of car with equal success, but his career came to a sudden end when he crashed at 31 years of age at Goodwood in a Lotus in an accident for which no-one has ever produced a rational explanation. He recovered physically but had lost the fine edge of the combination of abilities which makes a top driver, and did not want to be an also-ran. So he retired.

Although twin rear wheels were used on some Grand Prix cars for hill climbs in the 1930s, the six-wheeled car came to Grand Prix racing as a great novelty in 1976. Here the Tyrrell Project 34, driven by Patrick Depailler compares with the conventional Penske driven by John Watson in the Spanish Grand Prix

Two other young men who were Moss's contemporaries, Mike Hawthorn and Peter Collins, were both strong public personalities but not as professional as Moss in attitude nor perhaps as dedicated to the business of winning races. Both were killed, Collins in the German Grand Prix, Hawthorn in a road crash. Among other crowd favourites were Duncan Hamilton, a heavyweight sailor who won for Jaguar at Le Mans 24-hour race, and whose private antics produced several amusing books.

The professional driver really arrived on the scene and took over from the gentleman amateur after the Second World War, but Hamilton belonged to the earlier fun-loving era and was there to enjoy himself above all, leading to stern words from team manager 'Lofty' England of Jaguar who was certainly not there for fun but as part of a serious business enterprise. In spite of these divided motives Jaguar put up a record at Le Mans with five wins, a state of affairs not approached by any British cars since the Bentleys of the 1920s and 1930s.

Moss has a sister who after show-jumping victories with horses became a top rally driver, and Pat Moss then formed a husband and wife team with the Swede Erik Carlsson, commonly known as Erik on-the-roof Carlsson because of his apparent liking for inverting his Saab car in the course of rallies. Erik suffered such a pounding in rally cars all over the world for so long that his spine eventually objected and he now has a permanent stoop. At times he had to be lifted into his car but persisted in finishing the event. As he is a very large man his stoop looks ungainly, but he says he feels no pain and can live with it, as doctors can do nothing about it. He was born in 1929, the same year as brother-in-law Stirling Moss and was rallying from 1953 to 1964, when he married and faded out after a string of victories won in not very powerful cars.

Carlsson started a fashion for Viking drivers from Scandinavia which swept the field and led to statements from British manufacturers' rally team chiefs that they would never employ Britons again after the phenomenal success of all the Flying Finns–Aaltonen, Makinen and company–but one Englishman can still keep up with the best of the Scandinavians. Roger Clark has now become known to an even wider public by advertising hair oil on television while leaping his Ford through the air. Clark started rallying in 1961 and had little luck in his first years; his victory in the 1972 RAC Rally showed that he could beat the best of the Scandinavians, but the Ford policy of concentrating Clark's rally activities in Britain meant that he was seldom pitted against the top men on the international scene, such as Walter Rohrl or Sandro Munari, who was to drive the near sports-racing Lancia Stratos to victory after victory in major international rallies.

Like most of the leading drivers, Clark has his own technique of throwing his car sideways into a corner at apparently impossible speeds and angles, but it works. He tried to pass on some of his skills to Graham Hill who had been successful in most forms of racing and tried his hand at rallying for publicity purposes. Drivers are split on the merits of circuit racing versus rallying, depending largely on which one they are good at. Carlsson says racing is dull, 'Always going round the same bloody corners' and lacks the challenge of the unknown, although nowadays rally drivers practice as much as circuit men, even if they are not supposed to know where the route is.

left
The ebullient Mike Hawthorn
in Vandervell's Thin Wall
Special (really a Ferrari) at
Goodwood in 1953 in a
characteristic pose

above
Graham Hill on his favourite
circuit at Monaco, where he
won five times, in 1968 with a
Lotus 49

left
The long-time king of British
rallying, Roger Clark, doing his
sideways thing in his
always-immaculate Ford Escort
in the 1975 RAC Rally

Classic racing car of the 1920s
was the Bugatti Type 35

Roger Clark also gave some tips to Jim Clark, who took to
forest rough-road driving more readily than Graham, although
he went out of the RAC Rally after three accidents. Jim Clark
should need no introduction, any more than his compatriot
Jackie Stewart, son of a Scottish Jaguar dealer. Both men showed an inborn natural talent at the wheel of a racing car and
rocketted to the top of their profession. Clark was a sheep-
farmer's son and began driving in races when 20. He became
world champion, won Indianapolis and was invincible most of
the time, yet always quiet and unassuming. He died in an un-
explained crash in a minor Formula 2 race at Hockenheim,
Germany.

Stewart was also a top-flight driver and a crack shot but a more
extrovert personality and is still involved in all kinds of business
enterprises. He began racing in the shadow of his elder brother,
but rapidly became his own man and was three times world
champion before retiring.

There have been so many good drivers in the history of the

Classic of the 1930s was the Alfa Romeo Tipo B, the first true single-seater Grand Prix car

many branches of motor sport, some killed in their prime, that we can only look at the surface of the pool and see where it shines brightest. No pool of experts will agree on rankings, but three of the greats already mentioned will be on everyone's list: Nuvolari, Fangio, Moss. Many others can be added for different reasons, and if we take a quick alphabetical look at the roll of honour then the Ascaris, father and son, must rate a mention. Alberto was only seven when his father, Antonio, was killed at the Montlhéry track, but he followed on and took the world championship twice in Ferraris; he too died testing a Ferrari at Monza.

Three Bentley drivers from the sports car racing days thrust themselves forward too: Woolf Barnato, Dr J. D. Benjafield and Sir Henry Birkin. Theirs was another world in which the cars they drove bore some resemblance to road cars, and in the early Le Mans days had actually to be driven part of the distance with their rag-hoods up, and carry all spares and tools on the car. They made as big a name at play as at work, and The Bentley Boys could have filled many books to themselves. Speculation is always with us as to whether the top drivers of past eras were better than the best men today, but it will always be an unresolved argument as we have no basis of comparison. Modern cars are certainly easier to drive and a moderate performer can achieve a reasonable level of competence, which might not have been possible on the machine of years ago, but it is the fifths of seconds off the lap times at the top end which become more and more difficult to achieve except by the absolute masters, who are still a small band.

Australian Jack Brabham should have a niche as he could break all the rules and still win, the rules that is which govern the behaviour of other people's cars. But Jack came from the

Another one of the greats, Jim Clark after one of his many wins for Lotus in the Dutch Grand Prix of 1967. This was also the first victory for the Ford-Cosworth DFV engine, which was still winning Grands Prix nine years later

dirt-tracks and threw his machine around with tail-sliding abandon until he refined his technique and began to conform, more or less. But he won races, was world champion, rarely crashed or was injured, and retired full of years and victories at 44 after driving in 127 ranking races. 'Black Jack' could be monosyllabic and taciturn, but he was a professional. He also became a highly-successful constructor and the cars in which he won his third world title (in 1966) were Brabhams.

The outstanding New Zealanders were Denny Hulme, who drove Brabhams to win the championship in 1967, and Bruce McLaren, who won championship races but never the championship. However, he founded the widely successful McLaren firm and teams, which took the CanAm championships with almost insolent ease year after year, the Indianapolis 500, and the world championship with the talented Brazilian Emerson Fittipaldi.

Fittipaldi had gained his first championship driving in Colin Chapman's Lotus team, in cars painted in the colours of a Player's cigarette brand and even named 'John Player Specials' in one of the more extreme examples of the sponsorship which had become essential to any form of motor sport at the top level in the 1960s and 1970s.

A few Americans crossed the Atlantic over the years to battle in Continental races, just as some of the early birds went to Indianapolis from Europe, with some success as the records show. But later the 500 became virtually an all-American affair until Lotus made their successful bid. Those who made their mark in road racing included Masten Gregory, A. J. Foyt, Dan Gurney, Ritchie Ginther, Andy Granatelli (as entrant) Mario Andretti, Phil Hill, Carroll Shelby. But the interchange has always been on a small scale until more recent times, as the sport has developed in different ways in the two spheres of activity.

Several men have made their mark both on two wheels and on four, notably Nuvolari, Rosemeyer, Jean Behra, Mike Hailwood and John Surtees, who has been world champion in both spheres, but the techniques and requirements are different and not many have recently been able to make the transfer with success. Top-flight motor-cycle aces say they feel too remote from the road when encased in a metal box, and another complicating and perhaps more important factor is that the racing line through a given corner is different on four wheels from the right one on two, which can lead to what might be called difficulties.

Women drivers of great ability have also been thin on the ground but it must be faced that in former years it was much more difficult for them to break through the established barriers, and it may be not so much that they did not exist than that it was too difficult for them to find a drive. Some did succeed in spite of all this. Madame Camille du Gast makes the point; she was the first woman to drive in major events, as early as 1901 in the Paris–Berlin, and also competed in the ill-fated Paris–Madrid of 1903. She drove big heavy cars which we would call 'hairy' today, but made no concessions to her sex or 'frailty'. But in 1904 women were barred from the big events and that was that, although she went on to drive power boats.

The other great name from the early days is of course Elizabeth Junek from Prague, who came later and first came to notice in 1924. She was born in 1900, yet as recently as 1969 she drove a Bugatti at a historic car meeting at Oulton Park in England. She made her mark in such events as the Targa Florio in Sicily and the German Grand Prix over the then new Nürburgring in 1927 when she won her class in her Bugatti. She gave up when her husband was killed in the following year's German GP.

Gwenda Hawkes made a special mark as she drove not only cars but motor cycles and three-wheelers as well, from 1922 until 1939. At one time she held the ladies' lap record at both the English Brooklands track and at Montlhéry near Paris, where she made her racing home under the banking. Petite Kay Petre belonged to the same era. She achieved passing popular fame by being dipped in a bowl of plaster of Paris to make a mould for a rubber seat insert so that she could see over the cowl of the 10·5-litre Delage in which she did a 134 mph lap at Brooklands.

In more recent times, the barriers to women have not been so daunting and we have seen many competent performers both in road and circuit racing and rallying. Lella Lombardi, who drove a Formula 1 car in the March works team, and scored in the 1975 world championship. But it is in rallying that woman have reached equality with men, never more so than in 1960, when Pat Moss drove an Austin-Healey 3000 to win the demanding Marathon de la Route outright.

In the 80 or so years that motoring competition has been going on, less breaks caused by wars, some 400 drivers have achieved fame of varying degree, broken records, been in works' teams, or made a name for some specific contribution, if only performing in a competent way over a number of years. Inevitably many names have been left out in this brief attempt to recall the flavour and variety of the sport rather than to give a complete record of all that has happened, so no-one should feel aggrieved if their favourite has been pushed out by the physical limitations of space.

Jackie Stewart, the one who survived, and was an undisputed master, at the Dutch Grand Prix of 1969 in a Matra, followed by Graham Hill and Denny Hulme

Motoring for the Masses

There is a paradox in the fact that whereas the first cars were handbuilt objects for the enjoyment of the wealthy few, we have now reached a stage where the only way that a manufacturer can survive is to make enormous numbers of more or less identical vehicles, unless he is engaged in the rarified atmosphere of making a few expensive machines, which fewer and fewer companies are able to do and survive.

We have already looked at the Model T Ford, the Austin Seven and the Citroën 5CV, which were pioneer 'cars for everyman', but these were overtaken later by the Volkswagen Beetle, which was made in even larger numbers than the Model T and in a much shorter space of time, and later still by many other models, although none of them to date have achieved the 15 000 000-plus production run of the T or the Beetle.

Ford was the first man to go for the mass market but his example has since been followed by exponents of every possible configuration of motor car, from the classic layout of the Austin Seven with the engine at the front driving the rear wheels to what we must call the Mini layout with the engine at the front driving the front wheels. In between we have had the example of the enormous success of the Beetle, with its engine at the back driving the back wheels, so the only thing left to be tried is the mid-engine, which is not suitable for a four-seat passenger car, or a rear engine driving the front wheels, which would not appear to make much sense unless some new truth is discovered.

The split between Europe and America, with cars on one side of the Atlantic getting bigger and bigger while those on the other side were shrinking makes it difficult to consider the history of both together. But although the United States is the home of the biggest markets, its domestic cars have tended to be similar in concept and layout, once the initial wierdies had died out, and apart from the odd freak or non-conformist here and there.

This is not a dismissal of United States production over the years as of no interest, but an admission that it tended to less variety once the pattern was established and did not produce all the varieties on a theme which we have seen in Europe. Americans may throw up their hands in horror and say what about so-and-so which was air-cooled or all made of aluminium or cost a million dollars or had this or that marvellous attributes, but they are not the mainstream output typical of their origin.

One of the first people after Ford to try to bring the car to the people, if we ignore the post First World War horrors in the shape

above
Japan copied the Austin Seven but made it grow up a little. This 1932 Datsun shows how it was done

opposite.
The American Willys shows off the typical roadster form of the between-wars period

opposite
GN cyclecars—this is a 1914 Grand Prix model—survived in production longer than most of this curious breed

Ford's Model A never quite
had the magic aura of the T,
but was a good workhorse of
the early 1930s

of cyclecars made of string and sealing wax, was Leslie Hounsfield the Trojan man, who sold under the slogan: 'You can't afford to walk', on the premise that shoe-leather cost more than the running costs of his rather odd motor car. People who can remember the Trojan today will probably recall the red vans used for so long by Brooke-Bond's tea, put-putting about the place and in no danger of prosecution for exceeding the speed limit. The maximum was said to be 38 miles an hour, but hard to prove.

The Trojan was odd in every way and looked it, with its two-stroke engine under the seat. It suffered from a 12-year gestation period, so that by the time a 1910 design hit—if that is the word—the market in 1922 it was a bit long in the tooth. If it did not do much else it provided a lot of motoring jokes, including the one that if the disc wheels slipped into the tramlines you had to go to the depot. It lasted until 1936, and is not sadly missed.

There have, of course, been dozens of makes aimed at big-time production which disappeared more or less without trace and of which many of us have never heard. It seems incredible that 66 makes of British three-wheel car were offered between 1899 and 1964, the only survivor of this strange breed in production in the mid-1970s is the Reliant Robin.

But none of the three-wheelers ever achieved enough share of the market to qualify to be called a provider of motoring for the masses. In the between-wars years both Morgan, with one wheel behind, and BSA with the same layout, were seen about in small numbers but for the use of eccentrics, enthusiasts and masochists rather than the family man. Some of the other devices, one looking rather like a telephone box on the move, had better be nameless.

The next serious impact undoubtedly came from William Morris, arch-rival of Herbert Austin of Seven fame. He started in the bicycle business near Oxford, England, first repairing them and then producing bespoke models and racing them himself. He made himself a motor cycle as early as 1901, and went into partnership to make and sell them. Cars were the obvious next step and by 1913 he was assembling them out of other people's parts. Thus was born the Morris Oxford, although William set a much-copied fashion when his first motor-show car appeared with a wooden engine as the real thing was not ready.

The prospects for the 1018 cc Oxford (at £175) were put back in 1914 by the outbreak of war. Morris visited the United States and learned production-line methods, and ordered engines there from Continental for his planned post-war four-seater which was to take over from the two-seater Oxford. It was called the Cowley

below, right
William Morris' milestone, the Morris Cowley in 1926 period trim with running-board petrol can and full weather equipment, was better known as the Bullnose, made a lasting mark on the English scene

below
Volvo P4 typified middle-class European cars of the 1920s. Introduced in 1927, it had a 28 bhp 1·9-litre engine

above
Buick's 1918 Model E/645
was an open tourer with a
six-cylinder, 242 cubic inch
motor and the wooden-spoked
artillery wheels which tended to
persist in the States

left
The engine of the Buick E/645
showing the external pushrods
and long ancillary drive to
water pump, distributor and
so on

when it came in 1916, and he even managed to make it during the war. Morris survived all sorts of crises to make cheaper and smaller cars, challenging Ford's T on the British market, until he eventually–and briefly–got the price of a sparse version of his baby two-seater Minor down to £100.

The famous Bullnose Oxford and Cowley had founded his fortune, but it was the later models like the Minor of the 1930s and the Morris Eight which ran up to 1938 which spread the popular motoring gospel to the people. In other countries people like Renault, Citroën, Opel–all great names from the early days–were following the same trail but none of them made money like Morris or had such a big influence on the trend of car design and production in Europe, except perhaps Citroën who like Morris had espoused the pressed-steel body and also made front-wheel drive respectable. Morris sold a quarter of a million of his Eights, which may be small fry against 15 million model Ts or Beetles, but he did it in four years.

We must follow his fortunes a little longer as he also influenced much later developments in the mass-motoring industry. One of his employees had been Leonard Lord, another fiery figure like Morris himself, who left him after a row to join Austin. Lord threatened to get back at Morris and did so by influencing the formation of the 1952 British Motor Corporation, which ended Morris' independence. Meanwhile, the second model under the Morris Minor name had appeared in November 1948, the bulbous district-nurse car which was so novel in its day with torsion-bar suspension and rack-and-pinion steering. Morris himself had little to do with this car, which came from the drawing board of Alec Issigonis, whose next step to the Mini was the one which gave the language a new and now tedious word. But a million and a quarter Minors were sold before the Mini came.

The Mini must be a star of the story of motoring for all, as its small size, initial low cost and all the other attributes of the car-for-all made it an inevitable winner once public reaction to something entirely new had been swung round from resistance to enthusiasm by clever publicity means. These included equipping several leading motoring writers with the new midget so that they would be seen about in it, and putting Grand Prix drivers in them for circus-style races, in one of which the elfish Innes Ireland persuaded everyone to shoot off backwards when the flag fell.

Not much new can be said about the Mini, which has now had its day and been overtaken by other people's ideas, although still very much a best-seller. But its influence on the evolution of the motor car has been as great as any design ever produced. It sold to the public the tiny-sized car, the tiny road wheel, the tiny engine, a novel suspension system with no steel springs, and the concept of no wasted space. Its forerunner in some ways was the Fiat 500 of 1936; although accepted in its native Italy the baby Topolino (mouse) was always something of a freak elsewhere for those who wanted 'something different' rather than an everyman's practical transport.

It did not for one thing, offer the speed and acceleration which came with the Mini, 23 years later, or the accommodation, although it did have fuel economy on its side. It must rank, though, as a serious attempt to bring the car to the people, even if its original two-seater format and sluggish performance put it out of court as a serious contender for the family transport role. It held a parallel standing to that of the earlier Austin Seven, which catered to a certain section of the market but never ousted

above
Morris' £100 two-seater Minor of the 1930s undercut his rivals and caused a motoring revolution like his successor's Mini

above, left
Citroën's Light Fifteen surprised the motoring world with its front-wheel drive and toughness on rough going. This is a post-war version of the 1936 model driven by J. Van Ness in the Tulip Rally in 1950

left
Citroën took the bull by the horns and adopted the American Budd's all-steel one-piece body in 1925. Here B14s are coming off the line at the Quai Javel factory

the full-sized car. Oddly enough the 596 cc Topolino pushed out the same miniscule amount of power—13 bhp—as the Austin Seven of 1934.

Now that all major European manufacturers are turning out small cars in large numbers it is impossible to single out one make or model as the People's Car. Contenders for the role who now have to be considered are the Japanese manufacturers, who were the last to come to market yet have managed to dominate much of it with cars which may not be technically the last word but please enough of the people enough of the time to make them very profitable and leaders in their field.

The first post-war Japanese efforts were with puny cars of the order of 350 cc, of which there was an infinite variety of models not so many years ago. The technological and economic revolution which has turned a national industry from midget-makers to world leaders in sales of popular models needs more words and space than we have. The German industry performed a similar trick, in switching from strange post-war economy devices to lead certain sectors of the market today.

The other half of our picture, that of catering for the mechanical needs of Elegant Society, presents an entirely different but no less fascinating saga of machines made with more emphasis on suitability for their specific use than on cost, and with little consideration for the unfortunates who might have to clean, service and minister to them. Once upon a time the number of makers catering for the carriage trade was legion—there were more than 20 offering electric carriages—and yet now they can be numbered on the fingers of one hand. There are virtually no independent coachbuilders left, as the few remaining are owned by or contracted to major manufacturers. If there are still exceptions, the number of cars they make, or bodies they fit, is so small that it hardly invalidates the argument.

Yet as late as the 1930s there were in Britain alone more than 40 coachbuilders offering more than 70 different body styles for the wealthy man who wanted a one-off. Admittedly some of them were different names for the same thing, but nevertheless all these different styles were listed, ranging from open two-seaters with all sorts of fancy names like Torpedo Cabriolet to formal closed coachwork like the limousine, which incidentally did not mean just any old big car but one with a glass partition between the chauffeur and the gentry behind.

Once the motor car was over its birth pangs and a working entity, the major makers offered their cars in chassis form to be clothed by the coachbuilder, who originally was just what the term says. It was many years before clever engineers discovered that nailing pieces of aluminium onto a wooden frame was a rather inferior way of making a body, but they had no other way to do it in the beginning, and the results often looked lovely even if they did not like rough roads and needed a lot of cossetting to keep them young and healthy.

The one-piece pressed steel body which killed the one-off is much stronger than the handbuilt piecemeal effort, although by one of those paradoxes with which motoring history is filled we have now reverted to making metal bodies out of a number of pieces welded together rather than from a single stamping as was the original mass-production idea.

Anyone interested in the coachbuilding art might like to know that the styles listed were: Torpedo, Landaulette, Cabriolet,

A rubber-burning Mini (Spice followed by Rhodes) at Brands Hatch in 1967 shows off the unplanned abilities of Issigonis' Mini Minor

Sedanca de Ville, Limousine, Sedancalette de Ville, Tourer Saloon, Two-seater Tourer, Coupe Cabriolet, Pullman Landaulette, Saloon Limousine, Brougham Limousine de Ville, Pullman Limousine, Torpedo Cabriolet, Enclosed Cabriolet, Three-quarter Coupe, Pullman Limousine de Ville, Two-four Seater Open Sports, Sports Tourer, Sports Torpedo Cabriolet, Sports Saloon, Coupe Cabriolet, Coupe Limousine, Two-door Fixed Head Coupe, Faux Cabriolet, Six-Light Saloon, Brougham de Ville, Sports Sedanca de Ville, Saloon with Division, Cabriolet Sedanca de Ville, Touring Limousine, Oxford Tourer, Piccadilly Roadster, Pall Mall Tourer, Salamanca, Berwick Limousine, Paddington Limousine, Convertible Coupe, York Roadster, Derby Tourer, Ascot Tourer, Henley Roadster, Town Car, Open Drive Landaulette, All-Weather, Two-seater Drophead, Two-door Saloon Coupe, Fixed-head Three-quarter Coupe, Drophead Sedanca, Two-door Sedanca Coupe, Two-door Saloon Coupe, Close-coupled Coupe, Four-light Limousine, Drophead Sedanca Coupe, Sports Sedanca de Ville, Double Phaeton, Salamanca

William Morris' 10 hp Model of 1913 with White & Poppe engine was the forerunner of the Bullnose

Cabriolet, Two-door Foursome Drophead Coupe, Concealed Head Cabriolet, Single Coupe Cabriolet, Single Cabriolet, Two-seater Boatdeck Tourer, Three-quarter Limousine, Golfers' Coupe, Saloon Cabriolet, Wagonette, Sedanca Saloon, Sporting Cabriolet de Ville, Fixed-head Cabriolet, Single Landaulette, Short-coupled Saloon.

Offhand one can think of the Owen Sedanca, which is missing, and of course the shooting brake, station wagon, estate car or break, which are all the same thing.

So catering for the rich was quite an industry diversified into many trades, using carpenters, panel beaters, trimmers and various other skilled men at a cost at today's pay rates which would put the whole operation right out of court. One of the last men to commission a really personal car must have been Nubar (Mister Five Per Cent) Gulbenkian, the oil magnate, who had a London taxi made into a many-splendoured thing. He said one of its virtues was that it would turn on a sixpence, adding 'whatever that may be'.

The great days of the limousine and the formal car were probably in the between-wars period, when a number of car makers like Rolls-Royce and Daimler offered their products as a very large chassis onto which the company of your choice would build any kind of design you required provided he approved. Car makers had suffered from time to time from over-enthusiastic clients or carriage makers who built such massive heavy bodies that the performance of the car became miserable and it was also liable to roll more than was desirable and upset the demeanour of the noble occupants.

But the sort of customer the companies liked were people like the old Duke of Bedford, grandfather of the present one, who kept formal cars at both his country seat, only some 40 miles

above
The big American car has often been widely different to its European counterpart. This is a Hudson 1916 town car, posed in a formal garden with Negro chauffeur and footman

top
The Rolls that didn't sell: the Brewster-bodied American-built Phantom 1 speedster-phaeton looked pretty but failed to beat the snob barrier

from London, and his town house, which was always staffed, heated and ready but seldom used. His maxim was that a gentleman never travelled with his luggage, so that two cars had to be used, probably Rolls-Royce or Daimler, to convey the guest from London to Woburn. But there was a further complication in that he did not permit town cars in the country or country cars in town, so that the two London cars with the guest and his suitcase had to stop at Watford to transfer their passenger and his effects into two other large cars to complete the arduous journey.

That kind of conduct may have been exceptional, but it set the tone of the carriage trade, and no chauffeur in those circles would ever dream of putting a car into its garage for the night still wet, so it would have to be leathered down no matter what the hour or at what time it would be needed in the morning. There are stories told of exhausted chauffeurs, home in the early hours and due out early again in the morning, who tried to cheat by cleaning only the side of the car on which their employer got in and out, with a view to making good the deficiency in the course of the long waits which they knew would ensue in the course of the day's duty. But some were found out when the driver was ordered to wait and their man climbed in on the offside. The penalty was likely to be instant dismissal in those more disciplined days.

Chauffeurs also had to put up with a great deal in the way of discomfort. It was normal for most of the available space to be taken up with the arrangement for the seating of passengers, and the minimum would be left for the fixed front bench seat, which

left
The Big American, a few years on, but pretty much the same mixture. This is a Buick Model 50 seven-passenger sedan of 1928, with wooden-spoked artillery wheels and occasional seats

below
Elegance for the few exemplified in a 1952 Silver Wraith touring saloon with coachwork by Park Ward, posed in suitably formal surroundings

had to do for the driver no matter how big or small he was. His bench would also be upholstered in leather, as no-one worried too much about the shiny state of his breeches or how cold his anatomy might be, whereas the upper classes in the back would be seated on warmer Bedford Cord, if not something even more refined.

Fittings in the rear compartment of the carriages in question are a thing of beauty and a joy to behold, with silver flower vases, vanity sets, decanters of cut glass with matching drinking glasses, and all sorts of other foibles. It is only very recently that we have seen the term 'cigarette lighter' used in car catalogues; they were always 'cigar lighters' in the golden days, and fitted in the rear with the trumpet down which the chauffeur would receive his orders. Speedometers on the rear division so that an eye could be kept on one's man were also common.

The United States boasted some good coachmen in days gone by, although the attempt to build Rolls-Royces over there is generally conceded to have been a failure, some say because the Springfield-built model lacked the snob appeal of the British-built original. Certainly Rolls-Royce of America went bankrupt in 1934, but whether because of the depression or snobbery can not be discussed, perhaps really because of a combination of factors.

We have tended to concentrate on the English coachbuilders, in part because their work so typified the 'upper crust' aspect. The French of course produced the film star's favourite, the Hispano-Suiza, one of the grandest of white elephants, the Bugatti Royale, and Gabriel Voisin's sometimes idiosyncratic voitures de grande luxe (among them a model with a straight twelve engine). Among the exhibits which decorated the Paris Salons of the 1930s were Delages, Delahayes and the like carrying bodies from bizarre to elegant, some of the latter setting examples for post-war stylists.

Italy had Isotta-Fraschini, who were the first to put a straight eight into serious production, Belgium had Minerva, while in Germany firms like Horch and Maybach built some very imposing motor cars to keep the better-known Mercedes company.

Upper-crust American manufacturers were hard hit by the

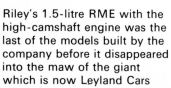
Riley's 1.5-litre RME with the high-camshaft engine was the last of the models built by the company before it disappeared into the maw of the giant which is now Leyland Cars

PXO 698

Depression, and few survived beyond the early 1930s. Some, like
Cunningham, Pierce-Arrow and Wills St. Claire, deserve to be
better remembered, for they built some extremely refined motor
cars, then there was Packhard (who had listed a twin-six at
$3 150 as early as 1915), Duesenberg and Lincoln, who produced
cars the equal of any in Europe, and sometimes in vastly greater
numbers.

The rules were the same whatever the nationality of the car
makers serving the nobility and gentry (as they so proudly
claimed) except that in some countries it was the aristocracy of
money which was provided for rather than the other kind. The
cars had to be big and gilded and opulent so that the owners
could be seen to be rich, although the old school eschewed the
vulgarity of the maharajahs' love of gold and mother of pearl,
outside spotlights which were also outsize for shooting tiger,
ostensibly, and such fripperies.

Some of the cars were of breath-taking beauty of line, even if
they were impractical in one way or another, and far removed
from the kind of mundane device with plastic seats and rubber-
carpeted floor which many of us are forced to drive simply as a
means of transport, unloved if not exactly unwanted. Even the
great cars were noisier, slower and less convenient to use than
the throw-away models which we use today, but they certainly
looked magnificent and mirrored the age in which they were used
by people whose last consideration was the cost.

Pictures tell the story of these behemoths better than words,
for grandiose appearance is their outstanding feature – parking a
21-foot Bugatti Royale on a meter in London would not be very
amusing. But then meters and such devices for controlling the
motoring of the plebs did not belong in the world of the carriages
of elegant society.

The Turbulent Thirties

A truly fast one and not a
Promenade Percy car, the
pre-war Brough Superior from
the famous motor-cycle maker.
The car had a big American
V8 engine

opposite, top
A star of the late 1930s,
BMW's 328 won races and
rallies and set the standard for
small sports cars of the era
and the post-war period

opposite, lower
Riley was a quality name and
the prototype 1½-litre Sprite
was one of their prettier and
more sporting models with
the high camshaft engine

The 1930s evoke a mixed bag of motoring memories. The decade saw many advances in the practicality of the motor car and increases in comfort, yet was in some ways sterile in major technical advance and saw the birth of some rather dreadful machines built down to a price in a bid for quick profit. This was the situation which in Britain led to the formation of the now-vigorous Vintage Sports Car Club in 1934, dedicated to the proposition that no decent car had been made since December 31, 1930 and that all vehicles built after that date should be ostracized by men who knew what they were about in motoring matters. They were deadly serious.

This period also saw the spread of controls on motoring. The first traffic lights had been introduced in Detroit in 1919, and the three-colour type appeared in Wolverhampton in 1928; now they began to come into general use. Speed limits in built-up areas became almost normal, roundabouts proliferated, in Britain driving tests were introduced in 1935. Whatever we may think of the cars it was certainly a time of milestones along the road of motoring history. Most of these things stemmed from the high rate of accidents, including fatal ones, which had come with the increase in traffic, and remained the worst totals for about 30 years, in spite of the much smaller number of cars on the roads. Those who thought like the members of the Vintage Sports Car Club blamed this on the poor design of current cars, but it is doubtful if this really had much to do with it; the upsurge in the number of cars about was a more likely cause.

On the credit side, roads adequate for the growing traffic began to be built – Italy had its first stretch of autostrada in 1924, Germany its first autobahn in 1935, and America had the Pennsylvania Turnpike by 1940. Most other countries had to wait until the 1950s for the beginnings of their modern road systems, and Britain's first motorway (the Preston by-pass) was not opened until the end of 1958.

It was the era when the two totally different kinds of cars, those made by traditional coachbuilding methods with a body consisting of a clad wooden frame mounted on a separate chassis, and those stamped out by American mass-production methods, were both on sale at the same time. Although André Citroën had started to mass-produce all-steel bodies in 1925, and his example was to be followed by other major manufacturers in Europe, the old ways died hard. One innovation as an alternative to the aluminium covering of the ash frame was the Weymann body from France, which used leather-cloth stretched over the

above
Best of both worlds: this 1938 Adler Trumpf Junior offered open or closed motoring at will

above, right
The typical 1930s sports car, perhaps better than most but also more expensive, the Aston Martin Le Mans as equipped for the Scottish Rally and Miss Kitty Brunell

wooden frame and was flexible, so that the parts of the frame could move in relation to each other instead of wracking themselves to pieces over the bumps. This worked well enough but cut-price copies which looked like the real thing but lacked its real virtues, gave the dog a bad name.

At the same time as there were various bids to make cars for the millions at a price they could afford, builders of luxury and sporting cars were reaching new heights of extravagance in spite of the after-effects of the great slump in the United States. The car was still bought by most people as a long-term investment to use for a number of years, which gave the builders of the more extravagant models a wider market when they had become slightly secondhand, making way for the next new one for the owner of the used model.

One of the effects of the invasion of mass-production methods plus the continued output of the old-style factories was that roads became quite inadequate for traffic, and the familiar scenes of jammed junctions and long queues to the coast and country joined the realms of everyday – or every week-end – life. Although people could now motor under cover in a saloon body if they wished, the 1930s were the heyday of the open touring car, when people used this bodystyle not because they had no option but from choice, most big makers offering both saloon and tourer bodies. Sports cars had become established earlier but were now available cheaply from many firms, of differing merits. Some of those now being preserved and restored as of historic value would be better forgotten and left to rust in peace.

The complaint then was that drivers could not use the potential of some of the genuinely fast cars available not due to the speed limits which inhibit us today, but because traffic congestion made motoring impossible for the sportsman. One of the problems of the normal family machine in contrast was that it was being made shorter in length, mainly for cost-cutting reasons, and the engine was being pushed forward to provide more room for the people further back. This did not help stability or handling, particularly when a laden luggage rack sticking out at the back tried to make the tail wag the dog which was already having trouble with its front legs. All the 'extras' being built in were adding weight, so the next step was to lower gearing, thus raising engine revolutions and producing the buzz-box syndrome which is the exact opposite of the slogging slow-revving progress so beloved of old-car lovers.

above
This 1931 Packard was a vehicle of high engineering standards with many detail refinements and good coachwork too

left
The Stutz Black Hawk was another costly model, whose name has lived on as a legend to many who have never seen one. There was a replica version in recent times

top
Elegance typifying the period.
Renault introduced their first
straight-eight, the Reinastella,
in 1929; this Reinasport
derivative, with Binder
coachwork, won the GP de
Grand Equipage at Nice in 1933

above
Kitty again, with the Talbot
14/45 coupe which she drove
in the 1929 Monte Carlo Rally.
Talbots had centralised chassis
lubrication so the oilcan is as
false as the hood-irons

above right
The Volvo PV36 of 1935,
reminiscent of the Chrysler
Airflow, had a 3-litre
six-cylinder engine and was the
first Volvo to have an all-steel
body

When these hard-worked little engines in the popular small cars were stressed even harder by the lower gearing, greater weight and growing traffic, they were made to produce more power by higher compression ratios and other means like multiple carburetters, and to conceal their staggering about under their burdens when running slowly the flexible rubber engine-mounting appeared to build in smoothness, as an advertising man might say. Many other devices came along, some more desirable than others, like the freewheel, the pre-selector gearbox and the traffic clutch, the synchromesh gearbox, the sunroof, automatic jacking systems, automatic lubrication systems for the chassis, which eliminated greasing, trafficators which preceded the winker, and flopped up and down to indicate a turn. They were sometimes inclined either to stay up or stay down and needed a thump in the behind, that is the back of the door pillar, to bring them into life. And if the car was going fast to make much wind pressure they tended to stay at half-mast, shining a feeble orange light from a feebly-dangling stance and confusing other drivers.

The synchromesh gearbox widened the horizons of driving by making it a possible pastime for those who could not co-ordinate hand, foot, and brain well enough to master the double-declutch and the crash gearbox, although there were many who simply banged 'em through without apparently suffering any pain from the unmusical clashings emitted by the mangled cogs.

Those who could not manage the one-two-three of foot and hand were now able to mask their lack of skill so that no-one knew. The pre-selector gearbox, originally designed by Major Wilson, appeared on many models—Armstrong Siddeley, Daimler, Riley, Talbot and so on—and involved a clutch pedal with a very strong spring. Strictly speaking it was not a clutch pedal but a gear change pedal, the method being to pre-select the gear required in advance and then actually engage it when needed by pressing the pedal down. But if one's foot slipped for any reason before completing the downpush, the large and heavy pedal would respond to this maltreatment with a hefty thump in the ankle which was most painful.

With a plain Wilson box one started off from rest by using bottom-gear band, but this tended to wear and become jumpy and rough in action, so various alternatives were tried. Daimler used the fluid flywheel, a fluid coupling as in a modern automatic transmission but with the third element, the stator, missing. This is smooth but very sluggish in take-off. Talbot tried another tack with Georges Roesch's so-called traffic clutch, which allowed the car to tick over in gear like one equipped with automatic transmission, then take off when the throttle was opened. It started to grip at 600 rpm and did so progressively up to 900 rpm when it locked to give normal drive. Unfortunately it was worked by steel balls running up and down, and when worn these could emit ear-piercing shrieks as if murder was being done in the car.

The principle of the epicyclic gearbox itself was not new, and had been used by Ford in his Model T and by others even earlier. The English Talbot company offered various refinements on the normal self-change operations, including one in which the box automatically pre-selected the next gear for itself as the previous change was made, and it was uncanny to see the selector lever jump about on its own as if operated by the invisible man.

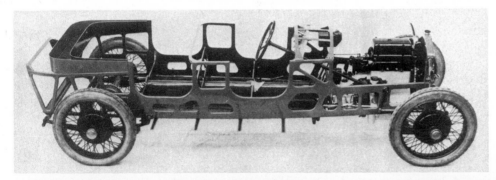

left
Lancia's Lambda showed how it should be done, with a chassis-body frame unit long before the Americans came up with the monocoque's predecessor 12 or more years later.

below
Four pre-war SS Jaguars lined up for a sports car race at Donington, their drivers without benefit of crash helmets in those unregulated days

The final refinement was for the box to start pre-selecting downwards when it had reached top gear, the only snag about all these refinements being that unless the driver had a very good ear for engine note he could never tell what gear he was in at any time, and was liable to make an expensive mistake.

Motoring in the 1930s conjures up a picture of a good time being had by all in the most jolly kind of sporting motor cars, but this was really a bit far from the truth in a time of economic blight in many places. This was reflected in the prices of second-hand cars, which were unbelievable by today's standards. Things like the flat-nose version of the Bullnose Morris, now a collectors' item, could be picked up even in the smart two-seater and dickey form, for about five pounds sterling in useable condition. They were really always in useable condition as they were rugged and simple to repair.

The British Government had earlier had a big influence on the design of engines in its own parish by introducing the horsepower tax in 1910 based on the RAC Formula, which took account only of bore and not stroke. This was always blamed for the production of the long thin engines which attempted to squeeze the best out of the rating from the driver's point of view by giving him the most engine for the least tax. Examples were the two-litre Lagonda rated at only 12 horse power, and the three-litre Bentley listed at 16 hp. Since 1921 the rate had been one pound per horsepower, which made big bangers a drag on the second-hand market, but in 1935 it was reduced to three-quarters of this rate, or fifteen shillings per horsepower, which lasted until 1940.

The British Talbot 105 finished in team racing colours from the 1930s. This car, shot on its way to Le Mans, impressed the experts when it ran there into third place in 1930–32 in almost complete silence

A chain-driven Frazer-Nash from 1935, a T.T. Replica, an anachronism which went on right up to the Second World War

This slightly eased the burden of the motorist, who in those days if he was an average man was talking in terms of running an eight, nine or ten horsepower car. Other legal effects came from the Road Traffic Act of 1930, which abolished the speed limit (20 mph) for cars and left the open road blissfully open until 1934, when the 30 mph limit was invented for urban roads. The 1934 Act also brought in the already mentioned driving tests to acquire a licence, and instituted the heavy goods licence.

This period also saw the arrival of what was called the arterial road and the by-pass around towns, the most famous in England being the Kingston By-pass to the south of London and the Watford By-Pass to the north. A notable feature of these roads and their counterparts outside of city limits of many American towns, were Road Houses, where a man and his girl could swim, dine, dance and drink without fear of breath tests. Perhaps this is what brings back a picture of jollity on the speed-free open road?

Most of us associate—perhaps as a tie with this carefree world—Bentley and Lagonda with the 1930s, although the old-school Cricklewood Bentley was gone by then. The period saw Lagonda move up from the beautiful-looking old two-litre, through the six-cylinder 16/80 which is rather frowned on by Lagonda men although just as nice-looking, and funny things like the Selector Special to the big Meadows-engined four-and-a-half litre cars and finally the 12-cylinder vee-engined machine of 1937, designed by Walter Owen Bentley after his own company had gone bust. People were rude about the Meadows and said it was a good engine for marine purposes.

The similarity in appearance between the touring-bodied
Bentleys, Lagondas and Alvises–which will of course be denied
by their respective fans–was due to the fact that the same
coachbuilders often built the coachwork, notably Vanden Plas,
a Belgian firm who moved to England in the 1920s and are now
part of Leyland Cars.

Talbot were also served by the same company but somehow
their cars look different. When we look at the catalogues of that
time it is an affront to the envious to see the variety of desirable
machinery which was on offer for prices which seem today to be
giving it away. Yet in fact although they were all such beauties
to look at and had a battleship gravity of movement past the
tiddlers they do not compare too well with the standards of ride
and handling performance which we expect now, and why should
they 40 years back? There are people who have made certain
modifications to engines, suspensions and brakes and persuaded
some of these old gentlemen of the car world to out-perform
their modern counterparts, but that is not strictly relevant to
what they would do then.

Ninety miles an hour was a respectable top speed even for an
expensive sports car, whereas we would find it hard to buy a
car today which would not do ninety, however cheap and nasty,
unless it were some kind of misfit. The Bentley which did very
much belong to the 1930s was the 'Silent sports car' which was
produced by Rolls-Royce after they had beaten Napier to the
buying of the Bentley firm, and was really a small RR with
twin curburetters. This one emerged in two forms, the $3\frac{1}{2}$-litre
and $4\frac{1}{2}$-litre, and finally with a geared-up top called the overdrive
model, which some say is the most desirable. In truth it made a
virtue of necessity, as so many owners were driving on the new
German autobahnen which Hitler had provided and ruining
their bearings by continuous high-speed driving that something
had to be done, and reducing the rate of running by higher
gearing was a simple way out.

But they were–and still are–very good cars to drive, and had
some of the loveliest-looking coachwork ever produced, allied
to good performance in silence and comfort and with reasonable
fuel consumption approaching 20 miles to the gallon.

A cat of another colour which must jump in late in the decade is what is now the Jaguar, a much respected animal, even if Bentley people were rude about it and said it was a Promenade Percy's car and call the original SS the Soda Squirt. The tale of William Lyons and his Swallow Sidecars has been often told, but his machine was significant as offering at a lower price than anyone else a product which had elegance of style and led to all kinds of developments, culminating in the XJ/S. From motorcycle sidecars he switched to saucy special bodies on Austin Sevens, Wolseley Hornets and such would-be sporting cars for those who wanted to look the part, even if those who could afford better things called the Hornet the Woolly Whore's Nest. So came about the SS Jaguar, long, low and not initially much of a goer with its Standard side-valve engine, but that changed later and it began to play the part as well as look it.

Another much fancied machine among those with sporting pretentions was the Lancia Aprilia, which came not long before the Hitler war and offered in a unit construction body handling and roadholding outside many people's experience. The Italian Lancia firm, now part of the Fiat empire, had long been pioneers, and used a pressed-steel frame on their Lambda in 1922, and also independent front-wheel suspension. In later years they tended to love complication for complication's sake, but in the 1930s they were leaders in machinery with sporting characteristics, and the Aprilia is still a sought-after gem for restoration.

There were so many sports cars from forgotten firms like Invicta and Lea-Francis and Sunbeam and of course Aston Martin who are still with us, although under trans-Atlantic ownership, that the driver-enthusiast suffered from an *embarras de richesse* and could satisfy every whim for supercharging or whatever his fancy was, even chain-drive on the Frazer-Nash right up to the war.

The more one turns it over in mind the more it sinks in that this was a glorious time for the sporting driver, even if the bread-and-butter cars in many cases left a certain amount to be desired. There were also more and bigger luxury cars ranging from the Belgian Minerva, 'the Goddess of Cars', through all the Ameri-

left
Luxury for some in the fastback, airline Austro-Daimler saloon of 1934

left, below
This 1935 Cadillac V16 still carried its luggage outside in spite of its luxury pretensions

can giants to the daddy of them all, the Bugatti Royale of which only half-a-dozen were ever made at £6 500–when a cheap car was costing £100. The princes and the kings failed to order this 125 mile-an-hour 13-litre giant, and Bugatti solved his problem by selling the engines for French railcars, which used a pair apiece.

Mercedes, the successor to the pioneer Daimler, were also making giant machines for the Nazi heirachy, which were some of the most imposing ever produced, mostly cabriolet style so that the leaders could be seen or stand up to review parades. With seven-litre engines they were fast in spite of their vast size and weight, although the supercharger which could be cut in at will was only supposed to be used for seconds at a time. Critics said it made a loud noise to encourage the occupants to think they were going faster, but did not affect the performance much, but this is a sour grapes-type comment from drivers of lesser vehicles. The size went up through the 36/220 to the 38/250 and finally the leaders' car the 540K, which fitted the image of military dictatorship with its aura of power and massive overkill.

Meanwhile at the other end of the price scale many of the small and cheap post-war cars from the 1920s had disappeared as their makers were forced out of business by the Depression, and there were not that many survivors to give a choice to the impecunious motorist. In England Austin and Morris were the domestic leaders, with Ford, now long producing at their British factory, challenging them with the Ford Eight and the egg-shaped Ten. Wolseley were a little more up-market and MG were making sports cars, long before they both became badge-engineered Morrises along with Riley, then also a slightly better class of machine than the Austin/Morris and in the Wolseley bracket with wood and leather and the air of a rich man's car shrunk to suit the worker's pocket, if it were deep enough.

In France and Italy the same names that we know today were filling the showrooms, Citroën, Peugeot, Renault, Fiat and Alfa Romeo, although the last named were basically sports and racing-car makers. France had some luxury cars like Delage and Delahaye but they were a declining breed as the world flexed its muscles for war and the all-conquering Germans dominated the motor-racing world, with their government's money behind them.

In the United States too the dozens of makes had slimmed down to the big corporations like Ford, General Motors, Chrysler Corporation and a few others, and badge engineering was the order of the day. Most of the experimenters like Auburn, Cord and others came to the end of the road because their machines were too costly for the times, and film stars and those who could afford to be way out could buy imported cars which were even more glamorous and unusual than the domestic product.

In England too many great names had disappeared; Sunbeam-Talbot-Darracq were all one under the Rootes banner and fading away in favour of mass-motoring devices like the Hillman Minx which offered what the man in the street would like to be able to afford, and came from the same stable, or at least the same owners if the breeding was not quite the same. Soon the Frazer-Nashes and Aston Martins would be driven by young men in RAF uniform on hard-found service petrol before being sold to the next man in the squadron by their widows as the war took its toll. The days of the open road and the wind in the hair were now to be spent in three-ton trucks.

opposite, top
America's fabulous beast of legend, the Duesenberg, which was bigger and dearer and faster than anything else— according to the mythology of the fan-club

opposite, lower
Largest production BMW was the 1939 3.5-litre 335, conceived as a high-speed long-distance touring car. This cabriolet version is preserved by BMW

Revival: Austerity and Flamboyance

When the world paused to draw breath at the end of the Second World War its motor industries could have drawn up a profit-and-loss account showing a very mixed picture. In Europe they had lost six years production and many of the factories had been destroyed. Their staff and workers were dead, crippled, prisoners or lost to other occupations. On the other side of the page some could show profits from building the armaments of war, and necessity had certainly been the mother of invention to produce mechanical novelties like the run-flat tyre, which enabled a gun tractor to drag an artillery piece out of action for a distance of up to 25 miles even if it had suffered a puncture. Curiously it was 20 years or so before the civilian world heard much more of such devices.

The picture in the United States was different, as they had suffered no bombing or destruction of factories and the economy was booming as a result of being the arsenal of democracy for six years although actively involved in the war for only four years. Some production of civilian vehicles had continued the whole time, but there had been little development of new models. Japan, now a world leader, was then unknown as a manufacturer of automobiles.

There was obviously a close parallel with the 1919 situation, when returning servicemen wanted to forget all about the past horrors and return to the land fit for heroes to live in which had kept them going in the mud and blood. One of the things they wanted was personal transport, and the motor industry was eager and willing to supply it. Unfortunately it was not too easy for them to do so; in England factories making tanks, bombers and other devices of death had to stop one job before they could convert to another. Raw materials were controlled by the government, and so was the occupation of people. Petrol was rationed, and was to stay that way for a very long time, far longer than anyone anticipated.

In 1919 the solution had been for a rash of small makers to burgeon overnight making curious machines known as cyclecars, which offered a cheap and primitive form of transport which would not have been acceptable to the England of 1945. This time the existing car makers scurried to get their plants back from the Ministries for whom they were making the war machines and to revive the production of designs which had gone out of business in 1939. In some cases military versions had carried on. Servicemen will remember the Army Model Austin Seven known as The Pram (short for perambulator or baby carriage), the Austin

Eight and other wireless trucks with an open back covered with a canvas tilt. Much favoured was the Humber Snipe, which had a luxurious car-type cab for two and with its aluminium cylinder head was no mean performer. 'Jeep' became a word in the international vocabulary.

Many army drivers had polished their skills on the Bedford 15 cwt truck, an open two-seater with an open rear which could also be covered by canvas. This was fitted with a governor to limit engine revolutions, but army drivers and mechanics with sporting inclinations soon learned how to 'tune' the governor. Surplus sales sprang up at Ordnance depots all over the country, and throughout Europe high prices were paid for anything that could move under its own power.

Pre-war cars were at a premium, and in view of petrol rationing the smaller-engined versions were most desired. The ration was supposed to provide the same mileage for all sizes of car, but if you could find a spare gallon anyway it would take a small car farther. The first European car back in production was probably the Citroën Light 15, a pre-war machine which had a high repute and was known as the Eleven in its native France or as the Traction Avant in tribute to its front-wheel drive, so novel when it appeared in 1936. In England Austin brought back their pre-war range of models as did most of the others, but some people had been busy thinking of the future during the war, notably Sir William Lyons and his Jaguar team who were soon to startle us all with a production two-seater with the unheard-of top speed of 120 miles an hour.

Citroën's 5CV cloverleaf seated three, two in front and one behind, and has become a firm favourite with the modern generation of students in France, although it belongs to their grandfather's time

Independent front suspension started to become more widely adopted in the 1930s, especially in America late in the decade, but although Vauxhall introduced it on a conventional popular model in 1935, such things were still regarded with suspicion in England – an independent front suspension design which Alex Issigonis had produced in 1938 did not appear in production until after the war on the over-heavy and under powered MG 1¼-litre saloons called the Y series, of which a few open tourers were also made for export. His first complete car, the Morris Minor, did not come onto the market until November 1948, after a good deal of argument with his masters. The stories have been often told of how they thought the car too narrow, so he sawed it down the middle and put another slice in, and of the lost battle for a flat-four engine when they wanted to use the existing and old-fashioned side-valve straight four.

In spite of all the compromises, the Morris Minor with its rack-and-pinion steering and torsion-bar suspension was a hit and set a pattern for others. There was not so much movement of cars between countries in the late 1940s, as each country needed its meagre output for itself, or to export in exchange for hard currency. One of the ironies of the age is that a team of British engineers examined the Volkswagen concept and factory, concluded that no-one could ever sell such a dreadful thing, and recommended that they give the whole horrid idea back to the Germans.

In France the Renault 4CV had been designed and put together secretly under the noses of the Germans who occupied the factory in 1942, and even given trials on the road. It was a two-door machine so like the Volkswagen in conception that there were rumours of copying, but the Renault team had never seen a VW when they laid their plans. Their new baby was of monocoque construction with the added novelty of independent suspension on all four wheels. The 760 cc engine was water cooled and mounted at the rear overhanging the rear axle, a feature of Renault design for some years and one which made them unpopular with insurance companies.

When the 4CV eventually reached the market, at the 1947 Paris Salon it had four doors, as Renault had decided that a two-door car would not sell. Louis Renault, founder of the company, had been dead for three years. He was arrested after the liberation of Paris in 1944, accused of collaborating with the Germans, and died from his treatment. Renault was a strong and self-willed man who refused to listen to advice and said, 'I have done nothing wrong. Justice will prove it'. It is a sad epitaph. He was always inarticulate and ill at ease with women and it is said used to ask them to go to bed with him as he could think of nothing else to say.

The Régie Renault, as it had become as a state-owned factory, also produced the Juvaquatre, a pre-war design not marketed until 1946 in small numbers. Another prototype, the 11CV developed from the old Primaquatre, was never produced although it was intended to compete with Citroën's all-conquering 11.

In Italy, Fiat and Alfa Romeo factories had suffered from bombing, and when they could tidy up enough Fiat went back to their 500, the two-seat miniature with a miniscule four-cylinder engine which had been around since 1934 and was modified in 1949 as the 500C, after a 1948 face-lift and switch to an overhead

valve engine. They made play with the fact that this model had 'a device for heating the interior of the car in cold weather'. The 1937 508C or Balilla 1100 was also back with us and went on for a long time as the 1100R. The 1500, a 1935 contemporary of the Citroën 11, was also soldiering on again in its famous pillarless saloon form.

These Continental cars all featured independent suspension on at least two wheels, yet were ancient designs. They fitted into the austerity aspect of the immediate post-war decade, when people wanted to pick up the pieces and resume their lives, and were not too fastidious about advanced engineering or the ultimate in performance as long as it was transport. Terrible mistakes were made in the scramble to push something—anything—which would sell onto the market, in which front suspensions had to be removed to get at engine sumps and similar absurdities.

MGs of three generations: in background a 1931 18/80 four-seater tourer, in the middle a 1934 K3 racer, and in foreground one the Americans loved, the 1954 TF (although the earlier T-types are even more popular)

If we accept that it takes five years to bring a design from the back-of-the-envelope conception to manufactured metal, then the timing is about right, for it was 1950 before the European industry was able to introduce truly new designs, apart from those mentioned which were hatched during the war. Fiat for instance introduced the 1400, which ran for eight years and was the first Italian car with chassisless construction welded up from steel pressings, if we except the Lancia Lambda of 1922.

Although 1950 is a reasonable date to take as that of the switch from post-war austerity to flamboyant materialism, no fixed time point can be put on a movement which starts and spreads and swells. But no doubt one of the foundation stones of the new generation was the 1948 introduction of the Jaguar XK120, which set standards of performance and breath-taking appearance not dreamed of before for £998 plus sales tax. Perhaps the brakes left something to be desired, like stopping power, but it was a great deal of smooth motor car for the money and a new concept among the pre-war designs which were being sold as current cars, *faute de mieux*.

Another illustration of the change of heart of tempo is that Renault, who had rejected the idea of a Citroën-beater based on the Primaquatra in 1945, reversed this decision four years later to produce the Frégate, which appeared on target for our time-sequence in 1950. The model is not one of those which will be listed by historians as great cars, but it was the first French model offered with fully automatic transmission, and a bigger and more opulent offering than the economy 4CV which had sustained the company thus far. Ironically, the director, Pierre Lefaucheux, who had survived Mauthausen concentration camp, died driving the car he ordered to be built.

Citroën were hitting back successfully at the Renault 4CV with their extraordinary 2CV, conceived in the late 1930s but introduced in 1948. This belongs very much to the economy era, although it was rejuvenated by the oil crisis of the 1970s and is still very much with us as a utility vehicle and the in-car for the young. In the normal car market Citroën relied on their ageing Traction Avant and its six-cylinder big brother until the introduction of the luxury shark-shaped D series five years after our time-point, in 1955. But then Citroën have always been a careful and cautious company who test everything to the Nth degree and beyond before they are satisfied that it is good enough to put on sale. Perhaps that is why they have always lost so much money.

The D cars belong very much to the era of luxury motoring even if they do not suit our time cycle, with their silent cruising, road-flattening suspension, and lack of wind noise. Only the clattering tractor-like engine spoiled the image. Everyone waited for the new engine, perhaps a V6 or V8, which never came, and now the car itself is out of production, killed by the rising price of fuel.

But in Germany, where we have talked only of the Beetle since the pioneer days, Mercedes epitomise the kind of motoring which we would all like to be able to afford. The really big Mercedes like the 540K have been mentioned, but their post-war successors beginning with the 200 series which have been successively modified while keeping a family shape right up to the modern S-class have always set a mark for others to aim at in the realm of luxury motoring. Admittedly they also make most of Europe's taxis and one snobbish motoring critic turns up his nose at

Citroën's answer to everyman's need for cheap transport has been the 2CV, shown here in its extraordinarily ugly 1939 prototype form (*below*) and as it was in production in the mid-1970s (*left*)

left
The shark-like D-series Citroën dominated the roads of France for a generation and was a car of the future with advanced suspension, silent travel and wind-cheating shape

below, left
The quality image of Mercedes does not stop them making most of Europe's diesel taxis. This pretty carbriolet A on the 220 series has classic lines which will never date

below
BMW's 328, here winning the sports car race at the 1938 German Grand Prix, was the foundation of their successful image on which they have now built an empire

Mercedes on the grounds that a gentleman does not drive taxis, but this is cutting off his aristocratic nose to spite his face. They do make some of the best, and improve them year by year. They are not cheap, but quality cannot be.

Their competitors, BMW, who used to aim at a more sporting market, switched their image from the 130 mph 3-litre coupé to the more economical smaller car in line with the world economic situation, but they did not make an impact in the early post-war era. Those were the days when the pre-war supreme sports car, the BMW 328, had gone and their business was in motor cycles

Two ends of the post-war BMW spectrum: their 1967 '600' four-wheel modern cyclecar with a motor-cycle engine (left) and the near-contemporary V8-engined sports car

and three-wheelers, and it was later, in 1961, that the foundation of the present successful series, the 1500, was introduced. But there was a brief excursion into the luxury market in 1951/52 with the six-cylinder two-litre 501 and in 1953/55 with the V8 503 and 507, a little after our set time.

Italy's sporting car maker, Alfa Romeo, was very much down on production after the war due to destruction of its factories. They had kept on making a few cars during the war, all of the six-cylinder Type 6C 2500 in sporting and touring form. The lowest point was 1944, when 18 cars emerged, and 1945 when they were down to nine. They began to pick up in 1946, still with the 6C 2500, which went on until 1952, joined by the 4C 1900 in 1950. These cars are not strictly relevant as they were the resumption of old models, and the modern and beautiful Giulietta did not appear until 1954. The 1900 was a landmark only because it was the first unit-construction Alfa.

The six-cylinder 2500 was not a car of the period as it was a hangover from 1939, but was good-looking, especially in some of its derivations like the 'Villa d'Este' coupé by Touring, the Pininfarina drophead, and 'Freccia d'Oro' (Golden Arrow) two-door saloon. They were comfortable touring cars with long torsion bars at the front, optional wire wheels, and the competition model offered 145 horse power at 5 500 rpm against the

The R-Type Bentley Continental. although it may look bulbous today, was considered a thing of beauty in 1953 and is now very much a collector's item

Alfa's first essay into unit
construction, the 1900,
unveiled at Rome presentation
in 1950 to President Luigi
Einaudi

standard model's 90 at 4 600 rpm. The steering-column gear-change was a little puzzling to those used to the orthodox as it was both back to front and upside down in relation to most others, with the low ratios toward the driver and upwards, making motoring musical.

In England the Austin A30 was running parallel with the Morris Minor. It was a tiny economy car, an up-to-date Austin Seven, which sold well in its day, but did not come on stream until 1951. Also of the time was the Austin A40, first of a long line with a Farina body designed in Italy, which appeared in 1958, after our magic deadline, but a trend-setter as there was a version with an opening rear estate-car style which became very much the latest thing in the 1970s.

The Standard company, which swallowed up Triumph and was then eaten by British Leyland, also went to Italy for styling inspiration from Michelotti. But their first post-war effort had been the razor-edged 1800 saloon, a scaled-down version of this called the Mayflower which was a bit top-heavy, and the pseudo-sporting 1800 roadster, a two-seater with a dickey or rumble seat behind. The year 1953 saw them produce the TR2, first in a long line of rugged, simple sports cars which sold well in spite of everything, like an engine developed to two litres from the old Standard, which was pushing things a bit, and a chassis from the same source which flexed more than somewhat.

There was also the Vanguard, which suited its times, a great bulbous saloon with many unpleasant features which neverthe-less sold well with a rugged tractor-like four-cylinder engine in an equally tough frame. In some ways it epitomised the post-war philosophy of making things the cheap way to work rather than to look nice. This was a 1948 debut, alongside the pre-war Eight which had come back until it gave way to the completely differ-ent monocoque Eight of 1954, which was peculiar in having no access to the boot except from inside the car. As the back seat rest hinged down it was useful for carrying items like a double-base with the front passenger seat folded, but a nuisance for the man who simply wanted to put his suitcase in from behind.

Much in line with the fashion for experiment which characterized the era, using Italian coachbuilders for design, bringing in the independent suspension long used in Europe and so on, was the Jowett Javelin from an old-established but now defunct company. It was all-new, a six-seater car which many thought handsome, capable of 80 miles an hour and 30 miles to the gallon, with a flat-four engine. It ran on in fairly small numbers until 1954, being joined by the sports version Jupiter two-seater in 1950, with a chassis designed by von Eberhorst of English Racing Automobiles. This had a chequered career, and the end came when Ford bought up Briggs, the firm which built the Jowett coachwork.

above
One of the Ferrari greats
was the Lusso, a road-going
gentleman's carriage which
could show a clean pair of
tyres to most things with a
150 mph top speed from its
250GT three-litre engine

right
Bentleys have always been big
and sometimes beautiful. Here
(foreground) a Derby snout of
what used to be called a
Rolls-Bentley in the 1930s
sits alongside a post-war
drophead coupe

left
Ford's British economy car of the 1950s, the 100E Anglia

below
Early Russian post-war car was this first Moskvitch, really a pre-war German Opel Kadett for which they had acquired the body dies

Ford themselves were not yet in the market position they command today, and made both economy cars like the first Anglia and Prefect, which are rudimentary by modern standards, alongside the V8 Pilot, a big saloon which used the small American V-engine of 3·6 litres which had been in army trucks and was not remarkably powerful, offering only 79 miles an hour top speed with a fuel thirst of 18 mpg if lucky. It looked remarkably like the American Ford V8 of 1932, and will not find a place in the hall of fame.

Another marque which has vanished, except in the field of armoured cars and light tanks, is Alvis. Much honoured before the war, they came back in 1945 with the TA14, a development of the 1939 12/70 which had really grown too heavy for its poor little engine. The same applied to the curvaceous 14, which eventually grew up into the prettier and more spritely TC21/100, still hampered by a pre-war gearbox which was not man enough for the new-found power. This was in 1950, and the Alvis is very much a car of the period when people would pay for something 'different', nicely tricked out in wood and leather, and not looking like the car next door. Their cars got bigger and some say worse until they were absorbed by British Leyland and ceased to make them. Their best model might have been the one which never appeared, designed by Alec Issigonis with a vee engine and all kinds of innovations, but it was considered too costly to build in the climate of the day.

The United States offered little which was original in this postwar period, as the cars were tending to be similar with big iron engines up the front driving the rear wheels, and even uglier than

below, left
Sporting version of the Javelin was the Jupiter, which was fine unless the cable-operated throttle stuck open. Racing versions ran at Le Mans and elsewhere and it had a purposeful air in its time

below
Jowett's Javelin was killed when Ford bought Briggs, the body-builders. It was an advanced small car, mourned by many

The Indianapolis 500, which had begun in 1911, was still packing them in the 1960s, as this 1961 shot shows, with the pace-car leading the pack to the start. A. J. Foyt won in the Bowes Seal Fast Special at 139 mph, but further back in the pack came Jack Brabham in a rear-engined Cooper, which was the first rear-engined European car to make an impact at 'The Brickyard'

ever as stylists ran wild. But much development work was going on in the field of creature comforts, like automatic transmissions, air conditioning, suspensions and braking (not before time), although the Americans were slow to take to improvements like the disc brake which were universally accepted elsewhere. The small-car invasion began with college boys and returning service personnel taking to MGs and Beetles, and the VW Beetle was later to head the charts of imports for many a year until the Japanese began to make an impact on the market.

The first five post-war years saw the weeding out of some unprofitable manufacturers, the resurgence of the Germans from the ashes of their factories, the beginning of the death-throes of the cart-sprung rear axle, many changes in materials and methods of manufacture, and demands from the buyer for more sophisticated equipment. It is odd that some best-sellers hanging on from 1939, like the Citroën 15, still offered virtually no space for luggage under cover. That was no longer good enough.

The Changing Scene

If we look at the evolution of the motor car chronologically, which is as sensible a way as any, the 20 years from 1950–70 saw an improvement and refinement of the man-in-the-street's car which had not been paralleled since the earliest motoring decades when engineers were simply struggling to make things work. There is a parallel here, as in our 20 years many ideas were perfected and made to work in the cheapest machines instead of being confined only to expensive small-production models, which in some cases now lagged behind their poor relations. An example is the disc brake, long scorned by Rolls-Royce yet used by the Fords of this world, and there are many other minor matters in which John Doe was being better served than his master.

By the end of our period, in 1970, the small mass-produced car would produce around 90 miles an hour from 1100 cc, give a good comfortable ride, handle like a sports car of not long ago, be heated or cooled and couple with these creature comforts the practical virtues of demisting and heated rear windows, all to be added to the benefits of infrequent servicing intervals and reliability. Perhaps the last Achilles heel to be tackled by the popular makers was that of the demon rust, and certainly the mass-produced cars of today are longer-lasting than their forebears of those earlier years. Some models were notorious for melting away before their anxious owners' very eyes, and the size of the company and its engineering staff was no criterion, as a glance at some Vauxhall models from General Motors would show.

Public opinion made itself heard in this regard, expressed through the power of the purse, until all the big manufacturers put their houses in order and also amended guarantees to back their claims. Right up to 1975 some makers were offering only six months (or 6 000 miles) warranties on quite expensive cars, which was somewhat unrealistic. But once a lead had been given others followed and most firms today offer unlimited mileage and at least 12 months time. Back in the 1930s Bentley offered five years, and the warranty could be passed on to the new owner if the car changed hands, so progress has been slow.

What are the fascinating aspects of this period? In all honesty the cars of 1950 were a bit of a mess in most cases, either hang-over designs from pre-war days patched up for a quick sell, or not very inspiring warm-overs of earlier thoughts. If we were to take a comparative catalogue of various makes of 1950 and 1970 and compare the models offered from the same sources it would provide something of an eye-opener. If we start with Britain and at

When the Volkswagen Beetle began to lose friends, the company's fortunes revived with the advent of the new-phase Polo (*top, right*) and big-brother Golf (*top, left*)—known in the USA as the Rabbit—which switched to front-drive and water-cooling

above
Basic shape of Citroën's *traction avante* models was familiar on the roads of Europe for decades after the first model was introduced in 1934. This is a late version, the 1954 15CV Six with hydropneumatic suspension

In their post-war range, Renault stayed faithful to the rear-engined theme until such models as the R4 and 16 were introduced in the 1960s. Typical rear-engined models were the 4CV (*right, above*) and the Dauphine, seen here (*right*) in its Gordini variant

the beginning of the alphabet with Austin for instance, the 1950 typical offering for the mass market was the first A40, not the Farina design (which came later) but the two-door Dorset and four-door Devon models, which would hardly win any beauty contests. They were admittedly an improvement on the pre-war designs like the old Austin 16 which had been sold five years before, but were soft, wallowy and imprecise in handling, offered only 40 bhp from 1200 cc, with a maximum speed of 70 miles an hour and acceleration over a standing quarter mile in 24 seconds, and there was not that much room inside.

A so-called Sports version of the A40 produced an extra six horse power largely from twin SU carburetters in place of one Zenith instrument, and Alan Hess drove one round the world in 21 days to demonstrate something or other. He chose a route a large part of which was over water, where the car nestled inside an aeroplane while mechanics ministered to its slightest whim. Brakes on the A40 were a combination of hydraulic and mechanical, which makes strange reading.

Now if we move on to 1970 a comparable car might be the Maxi, as Austin are now part of Leyland Cars, formerly British Leyland, formerly British Motor Corporation, and this with admittedly nearly fifty per cent more engine offers nearly 90 miles an hour, much more room, and slightly worse fuel consumption. But it has a five-speed gearbox offering relaxed high-speed cruising, better handling and brakes and many more amenities. It also costs a great deal more, but we cannot compare prices because of the drop in the value of money and rise in standards of pay and living. The Austin 1300 might offer a closer parallel, with its engine closer in size to the A40 at 1295 cc, and this one has the fancy inter-connected Hydralastic suspension system, much more interior room and performance, and certainly better handling from its front-wheel drive. Some people like to divorce roadholding from handling and treat them as two different aspects of the same thing, in which case we should also say that the roadholding is infinitely better with the smaller wheels, lower unsprung weight and wider-section tyres.

The same story will emerge if we compare like with like from any of the big makers except Volkswagen, who were still making their familiar Beetle although they had added other models to the range. None of these—the 1500, the K70 and others—met with

Volkswagen's Beetle hit the market in 1945 when the British had inspected the project, concluded that it would never sell and that the Germans could have it. They sold 15 million plus to make it the world's best-selling car, still going strong

99

anything like the success of the old people's car, and their fortunes were very much on the wane until the take-over of Audi
and the introduction later on than the period under discussion
of the Golf and Polo models which, like the K70, abandoned the
old air-cooled rear-engine concept.

Renault in France toyed with the idea of a scaled-up version of
their toy-like 4CV in 1949, but this was abandoned in favour of
the Frégate, the first mass-produced French car with all-round
independent suspension. They built a new factory at Flins, 25
miles from Paris, for the new project, designed to produce 400
cars a day, half the rate at which the 4CV was coming out a few
years later from the old Billancourt island factory started by
Louis Renault 60 years before. But a new star was in the wings,
slightly more grown-up than the miniature 4CV, in the shape of
the Dauphine, which was born in December 1955 out of the
talents of three factories, Billancourt, Flins and Le Mans.

The rear-engined rear-drive Dauphine went on to make history
with class victories in international rallies and enormous sales
in the United States until 1960 when the market suddenly collapsed and 60 000 Dauphines stood around on open air parking
sites slowly decomposing. The 4CV lasted 16 years and just over
1 100 000 cars were made, and the Dauphine topped 1 500 000
sales, but they were the end of an era for Renault, which now

performed a complete *volte face* from rear-engine rear-drive to front-engine front-wheel drive in the new generation R4, R8, R16, which restored the company's prosperity and were much better-handling and safer cars.

In the million-cars-a-year league Fiat and Volkswagen were competing with Renault worldwide, and in 1950 each had a different working concept as can be seen from their models. Fiat were classic-orthodox with front-engine rear-drive in the 1400 and the ancient 500C, but were to undergo two complete changes of engineering philosophy before the 1970s. First they followed Volkswagen with the rear-engined rear-drive 600, the elder brother of the 500, and then followed suit with the new 500 which had the same layout, which was air cooled although the 600 used water cooling. The New 500 sold more examples in ten years (1957 to 1966) – a total of 1 500 000 – than the old Mouse had done in nearly 20 years, a total of 550 000 between 1936 and 1954.

Then Fiat turned to orthodoxy again with the 1959 models 1800–2100, and in 1961 with the best-selling 1300 and 1500, then reverted to rear-engine again with the popular 850 series, trying orthodoxy once more with the 124 and 125 before settling on the front-engine front-drive layout of their more modern 127 and 128. But at the same time they were using rear-engine rear-drive on the puny 126, and classic layout on the bigger saloons (131 and 132) which might be called playing both ends against the middle. It is not possible to conclude which is the most successful formula from a sales viewpoint because of all the variables involved, but the 127 and 128 are the big-volume cars.

Although the argument over the best layout is evidently not resolved and the statistics could be arranged to prove whatever one wanted, the period under review did see the coming and going of alternative methods of production to the petrol engine, which continued to reign supreme apart from the success of the diesel in certain markets, mainly that for taxis. Various people toyed with the electric car, but the lead-acid battery remained too big, heavy and cumbersome for general use, although Lucas had some success with electric taxis and delivery vans limited in utility by short range cost. Pending the arrival of an alternative source of electricity this type of propulsion is not likely to take off. In Amsterdam the White Car experiment of electric cars is still running, under a system which allows members of the club to take a car from a station with their credit card and drop it at another elsewhere in the city for recharging, but it is a pilot scheme and the cars fairly rudimentary and not cheap.

The Wankel rotary engine is another new power source which has not fulfilled its promise. Three examples are shown here: the first NSU/Wankel Spider; the production NSU RO80 which had seal problems; and the production Mazda RX3, which has been raced with some success

So-called jet or gas turbine propulsion appeared on the scene from the British Rover company who produced prototypes, one of them good enough to run in the Le Mans 24-hour race, but they did not come anywhere near production for various reasons concerned with cost, dissipation of heat and difficulty of control as there is a long lag in response to the throttle, both on opening and closing, which makes driving a job for a master. Steam was played with in various quarters, notably the state-owned British Leyland, but is even farther from reaching the roads than the jet car.

The two-stroke also died the death, killed mainly by its oily and smelly exhaust which could not pass purity tests, and by heavy fuel consumption, apart from noise, rough slow-running and other problems. It remains in motor cycles, although being ousted by overhead cam multi-cylinders. The turbocharger, driven from the exhaust, was also marketed by BMW, the British tuning firm of Broadspeed on Ford and Vauxhall, and the sports car producers TVR, but seemed more suitable for circuit racing than road use, when the narrow useful revolution range and violent cut-in make life difficult except for the experts.

The Wankel rotary piston engine appeared in various cars, notably the Japanese Mazda which had some sales success and some in modest competitions, but it also seemed a likely casualty of the American pollution regulations, heavy fuel consumption, and sealing problems. The NSU Ro80, pioneer production car in this form of propulsion, was warmly praised by all who used it but did not become a permanent feature of the production scene.

So the transformation scene over these 20 years hinges not so much on any exciting new form of propulsion or wizardry in transmissions, but on steady improvement of the orthodox to produce higher standards in roadholding, handling, braking and more recently fuel economy, which has taken precedence over performance now that the whole world except Germany has clamped down on high speed. In the sphere of braking there have been attempts by several specialist manufacturers to produce a foolproof system which would prevent wheels locking-up no matter what the driver does, but they are all too costly for immediate production and only the pressure-limiting valve for the rear wheels is in general use. Double and triple circuits with built-in fail-safe factor are common, and complete loss of brakes is a relatively rare experience.

left
Holland's DAF Company, now owned by Volvo, built the only European all-automatic car, driven by rubber belts with an infinitely variable ratio, and loved by the ladies. The first version is shown here

below
Colt's Lancer is a typical Japanese child of the new generation, with all the 'extras' thrown in and a performance/ economy combination plus ride to suit all terrain. It has won the tough Safari rally in East Africa

There has been some effort to get rid of the spare wheel, which was such a boon when first thought of, but now is just a space-stealing nuisance, and a handful of production cars have appeared with the Dunlop Denovo specified as optional original equipment. This permits the car to continue to run on a deflated tyre for long enough to reach a garage, so that there is no need to carry a spare. It tends to make the ride firmer, and as punctures are a reasonably rare occurrence has not taken the motoring world by storm so far.

Similarly in the field of transmissions the only significant change has been the increase in popularity of the overdrive or fifth gear, brought about by increased mileages of motorway being built in most countries except Britain, where growth is very slow, with a total of little over 1 000 miles compared with West Germany's 3 406, Italy's 3 163 and the 35 019 of the United States (these figures relate to the end of 1973, latest available at time of writing).

Automatic transmission, although steadily improved over the years with better and more refined control systems, smoother changes, part-throttle downshift, has never really taken off in Europe or achieved a penetration or more than five per cent or so overall, and was really hit hard just after our 1970 deadline by the increase in the price of Arab oil. Before that time it had begun to make more impact in Europe and more and more manufacturers took up making their own units, which depend upon big-volume production to make the cost per unit economic. It is significant that Fiat, one of the biggest makers, have never thought it worthwhile to make their own units, although the reason may be that Italy is the market the most resistant to automatic transmission. There is a feeling among Italian drivers that to take away a man's gear-stick is to deprive him of his manhood.

France has taken to two-pedal driving a little better, with all the Big Four (Citroën, Peugeot, Renault, Simca) offering it at the period, although Citroën now only offer a semi-automatic unit. In Germany the penetration is higher, with Opel, Mercedes and Volkswagen all making their own units and BMW buying from the German firm of ZF, successor to the Zeppelin makers.

The only really small car to sell in any numbers with automatic transmission has been the DAF, Holland's only native car built by a company taken over by the Swedish Volvo concern in 1975, and this is only because it is not sold in manual form so the buyer has no choice. It also does have the advantage of offering infinitely variable ratios with no steps, achieved by a system of pulleys which change in diameter to suit the gradient and loading on the engine.

But in transmission as in other aspects of the automobile at this time no genius has come forward with a brand new idea, and we soldier on with a refinement of the sliding-pinion gearbox described right back in the beginning as 'brutal, even if it does work'. It must be some kind of commentary that whereas in the United States 90 per cent of cars have automatic transmission and many drivers have no conception of how to operate a clutch and gear-stick, in Europe the proportions are the other way round and 90 per cent have never tried two-pedal driving. This is partly a rub-off from the smaller engine sizes in use in Europe which cannot afford to give any power away to stirring hydraulic fluids. General Motors achieved the original breakthrough by

opposite, top
The Rolls-Royce Silver Ghost went on for a long time, always eschewing front brakes. This splendid boat-bodied tourer was said to come from Schebera-Schapiro of Berlin in 1914

opposite, lower
Chevrolet's Corvette, the GM Mustang, weighs in with a big V8 engine to pull only two people and is a modern American classic

107

above
The Toyota Carina is a mid-
1970s representative of the
popular middle-price models
which put the Japanese
industry on the world map

opposite, top
The Aston Martin DB6 with
body styled by Superleggera of
Italy

opposite, lower
Jaguar's XJ6 was a milestone
in motoring history with the
'grace, pace and space' slogan.
It offered outstanding
performance at a reasonable
price before inflation hit so hard

making all cars automatic, like DAF, so that the buyer had no choice, unless he specified a manual option which was not too easy to obtain.

Tyre design has played a big part in the advances in road-holding and handling, with some cars even designed hand-in-glove with the tyremaker to suit a particular type of radial construction. Between 1950 and 1970 the crossply tyre took very much of a back seat except on the feeblest and slowest cars which were not too demanding on their rubber, but the bigger and faster beasts called for special tyres with higher ratings for speed, resulting in the classifications we have today limited in safe maximum speed according to the type of car. This has been a very positive safety measure as the driver can see at a glance without the need for specialist knowledge that he is properly equipped for the limits of his own machine. The legal ban on the mixing of types (radial and cross-ply) and the use of worn casings, which applies in most countries, has also protected the stupid driver against his own lack of knowledge or intelligence, which is more than can be said about some of the laws imposed on the motoring public.

Suspension and steering systems do not lend themselves to exciting publicity pronouncements, and improvements have gone on without much fanfare or trumpets, but if we drive a 1950 car and compare it with a similar model of 1970 the progress is obvious. Rack-and-pinion steering, the most precise method of control, has tended to oust recirculating ball and other systems, and the simple McPherson strut front suspension has also spread to many manufacturers. Gas-filled dampers arrived on the scene, but are costly and mostly used for racing or competition purposes rather than normal road use. Some makers, notably Citroën, Mercedes, and British Leyland introduced suspension by other means than steel springs, using gas, compressed air, or a combination of one or the other with hydraulics, but most of the world's cars continued to flex lengths of steel either in bar or coil or flat lengths to find their freedom from bumping.

Many makers disappeared from the scene and there were many amalgamations as the tendency went on towards the reduction of the world's car producers to the handful that has long been predicted by such knowledgeable authorities as Signor Agnelli of Fiat who sees the day when each major European country will have one major producer. Significantly even the giants like his own company were losing large sums of money at a slightly later stage and the production of automobiles did not seem a very desirable occupation for a company.

In Britain the 20-year span saw the end of many famous names, and we finished up with two American-owned companies, and two soon to be propped up by the government, and no-one else in a big way of business. There were some survivors like the Morgan company who just kept on making the same archaic cars for a public who want something different, and cannot make enough, but many others found the going too tough. The first big merger was in 1952 when Austin and Morris, rivals since the industry began, became the British Motor Corporation and we saw Austin, Morris, MG, Riley and Wolseley cars all become identical but with different labels stuck on in the guise of badge-engineering, until the last two vanished altogether.

Marque names had perhaps lost their magic as hitherto unknown names from Japan, seemingly as far away as outer space, came into the market place and outsold the familiar badges on their home ground. As we gained Honda, Toyota, Mazda, Datsun we lost Alvis, BSA, Standard, Singer, Sunbeam, Armstrong Siddeley, Bond, Berkeley, Gilbern, Healey, Lea-Francis, Sunbeam-Talbot, Marcos and many others.

The Japanese cars won a reputation for reliability and some sold with a very complete specification, with even a radio thrown in as part of the original equipment. Industrial troubles in the British factories seemed endless and insoluble, and only in the world of motor racing were British cars supreme. One new name came and stuck: that of Lotus, successful in Grand Prix racing and builders of cars for people who loved to drive.

Colin Chapman, known throughout the racing world as 'Chunky', was the presiding genius, and the cars moved steadily up-market in price and specification from the build-it-yourself Lotus Seven, a four-wheeled motor cycle in effect, to the Plus 2 and Europa which were costly and sophisticated, offering unmatched handling and roadholding with reasonable fuel consumption. Of all the small companies who came into the car-building business Lotus alone succeeded and remained under the same management and moved from one success to another with their Elite, Elan, Plus 2 and Europa.

The New Sports Car Breed

Motor sport began within a few years of the invention of the first motor car, with the Paris–Rouen 'run' of 1894. We may argue about which exactly was the first car made as there are conflicting claims, but for our purposes it is not that important: what is important is that the idea of competition is nearly as old as the car itself. Men first of all competed on foot to see who could run fastest, then who could make his horse go fastest, then who could drive his motor car fastest and farthest.

So just as specialists bred particular types of horse for speed rather than strength and endurance, so the idea of finding that little bit of extra power to beat the next man is as old as the car itself. We have already looked at the definition of a sports car and decided that there is no such thing; we can not even agree on the title as the Americans call it a sport car when they mean the same thing. But there is no doubt in our minds as to what we mean even if we cannot define it and put it down on paper in an orderly form with which all would agree. Certainly race organizers have always had the greatest difficulty in composing a definition through which the competitors or constructors could not drive a coach and four. The classic case is the 24-hour sports car race at Le Mans in France, where the most extraordinary machines have been produced to beat the regulations, and have often succeeded in doing so as they complied with the letter of the law if not with its spirit.

There have always been two kinds of sports cars, those really built and intended for competition and the paler copies which a man may drive on the road and look as if he is going racing although nothing is further from his mind. Once upon a time we had appurtenances like chromium-plated stone guards on head-lamps, aero screens, and rear-mounted twin spare wheels on slab tanks to add to the illusion; the modern equivalent is the go-faster stripe and the spoiler.

But since we have had sports-car races as distinct from what we might call racing-car races, the sports car has at some periods been hairier and faster than its contemporary single-seater racer. and as far removed from something you could drive on the road as a jet fighter. If we ignore the monsters of the heroic age which by any definition were racing cars pure and simple, then the first of the latter-day racing sports cars were some Alfa Romeos and Bugattis and the 4½-litre Talbot from France, which was a hardly-disguised grand prix racer with two alleged seats. The Talbot, or Lago-Talbot, was unique as it started life as a sports car built for racing, with a four-litre cross pushrod engine pro-

ducing 165 bhp and using a Wilson self-change gearbox, made
in 1936 for the French Sports Car Grand Prix at Montlhéry,
where it did a record lap.

These cars went on to win at the Donington Park Tourist
Trophy in England, on a circuit which was out of action from
1939 to the mid-1970s when enthusiast Tom Wheatcroft under-
took the mammoth task of reconstruction. They also ran at Le
Mans and all the other sports car races up to 1939, then reappear-
ed after the war as single-seaters for the GP Formula of 4½ litres
(or 1½ supercharged). In 1948 they sported a new high-camshaft
engine with a claimed 280 bhp and went on winning races until
1952. In sports-car guise they won Le Mans in 1950 and would
have repeated this success the following year but for Pierre
Levegh's foolhardy attempt to drive the whole race single-
handed, a procedure which was later barred and drivers' stints
limited by regulation. Here though was the classic case of a

machine which began as a sports car, became a racer, and
finished up back in its original role.

Have there been any others? No similar car springs to mind.
There have been projects like the Ford GT40 and the Lola, which
were racing cars only, although there have been street car
derivatives of a somewhat limited usefulness for anyone who
aspired to keep his driving licence, although enormous fun while
it lasted. There may be some comparison with Jaguar or Aston
Martin, whose racing cars were somewhat different from the ones
you could buy but were nevertheless sports cars, and a Jaguar
C Type or D Type could be driven on the road with circumspec-
tion.

Looking at the catalogue of greats we might pick out Ferrari,
the daddy of them all in this double feature role of road and
racing car; Maserati, who played the same kind of part; Mercedes-Benz with the 300SL; Porsche, whose bread-and-butter

cars were rather different from the racers; and perhaps Alfa
Romeo with certain models. There have been others which certainly qualify like the already-listed Ford GT40 and the Lola,
and some doubtfuls like the Cunningham which really never was
and the Lotus Elite, purely a road car which was raced. We
might include the French Alpine, which doubled as a racer and
rally car, and if we turn back the pages of history a bit then
Bugatti and Delage are a must. But these great cars from the past
do not fit into the kind of frame we have in mind; nothing else
is like a Bugatti, which in its most popular forms like the Type 35
was a racing car in which one could go touring without luggage.

Machines like MGs and TRs do not qualify, worthy as they
may be as everyday hacks, as they were not in the big league.
Ferrari deserves first consideration, as he was really the founder
of the kind of machine we have in mind, built to achieve per-

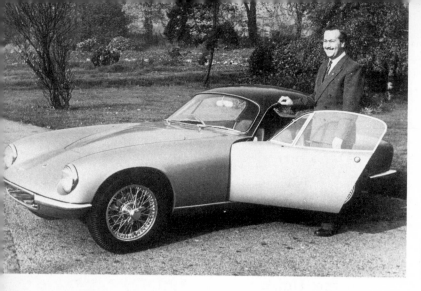

formance above all, to be unbreakable, to be its driver's servant, to be able to compete in anger if called upon to do so, or to give a boulevard ride if that was the need of the moment. Some models, like the 250GTO, did not qualify under this last heading as driven at low speeds an impression was that they were built virtually without springs, but let that pass for the moment. Enzo Ferrari must be unique in adding a word to the language – his name – when he began making cars only after the Second World War.

Enzo Ferrari was born at the same time as the motor car, in 1898, and at home in Modena his father was one of the first car owners. He saw his first race at 10 years of age. He became a test driver in Milan, then ran the Alfa Romeo racing team after a spell as a driver himself. Then he ran a nominally independent team of Alfas under the Scuderia Ferrari banner, using the prancing horse badge of First World War Italian air ace Francesco Baracca as his insignia, a black horse on a yellow shield, which the sporting world was to come to know so well.

Ferrari first announced his own cars in 1946, but they did not appear until the 1948 Italian Grand Prix in Turin. They were very small cars with supercharged 1500 cc engines, giving no hint of the monsters which were to carry the prancing horse badge later on. But Ferrari was impressed with the performance of the French 4·5-litre Talbots, and in 1950 his first 12-cylinder 3·3-litre GP car appeared and finished fifth in the Belgian Grand Prix on the Spa-Francorchamps circuit; later 4·5-litre versions convincingly defeated the then all-conquering supercharged GP Alfa Romeos.

The first sports Ferraris were sold in 1948, just two of them with engines of just under two litres. But although there were half a dozen early models like the 125, 166, 212 and 225, the first 'real' Ferrari known to most people is the legendary 250, which ran in the Mille Miglia of 1952. Then he began the trick of naming the model after the cubic capacity of one cylinder, which has persisted through most Maranello types. The Type 342, the Mexico 340 and the 375 Mille Miglia were true racing sports cars, and it is the 250, 275 and 330 types which were mostly sold to the public and are best remembered, although in between there were the 410, the 290, the 130/S56, the 315 and the 335, all different.

Twelve cylinders have always been the Modena sound, although there have been in-line fours and sixes, a V6, and a V8 as well. Ferrari history needs a book of its own – and indeed there are several books – but the road-going cars are a breed apart and offer a combination of noise and sensation that is unrivalled by any other machine. Rude people called the 330GT, which was large and heavy if only a two plus two, 'the bus' but it was still capable of in the region of 150 mph and tractable to boot. One of Enzo Ferrari's traits is that he is always more interested in the future than the past, and vintage-minded people who turned up at the Modena factory with old cars resented the lack of sympathy. He was more interested in selling them a new one.

When Ferrari's son Dino died young in 1956 much of his interest in motor racing, and in life itself, died with him. He ceased to attend races himself and relied upon reports from others. Writing about his cars himself in his memoirs Enzo said the SuperAmerica was the Chinchilla of them all, a V12 4·5 litre with enormous performance, made of course for the United States by Maranello. The dream factory has been under control of Fiat for some years and what will happen when 'the old man' dies is in the realm of speculation, particularly since the increase in oil prices killed the sale of such super cars.

below
Bentley claimed to be the silent sports car, but the Talbot went one better and won races in silence. This team of 105s taken in Nice before the 1934 Alpine Rally include BGH 23 on right, driven by Mike Couper, which is still racing

bottom
Porsche's road-going Carrera, not to be confused with the racers, is fast but civilized and shows how far they have come from the tubby thing made out of VW parts not so long ago

From the same neck of the Italian woods as the Ferrari came another post-war marvel, the Lamborghini, which has had a shorter life and is facing the same problems. The story goes that when Ferruccio Lamborghini, a self-made tractor king, could not get good service for his Ferraris he decided to make a better car himself, and that is how the snarling monsters began. Both cars have 12 cylinders, but there the parallel ends, for the Lamborghini was built to sell as a road car, has no racing background, and the factory have always turned their back on motor sport. Lamborghini himself has now sold out to a Swiss dealer. His car does not deserve a place in the roll of honour of sports cars which have won races, or fit into the Ferrari image, but it must qualify as a status symbol of the western world of the 1960s, on grounds of performance and handling as well as appearance.

Lamborghini began with the 350GT, then the 400, but it is the Miura, named after a fighting bull, with a mid-engine and a slippery shape, which put the company on the bright young man's map. Later came the Espada, the Urraco and the ultimate, the Countach, an untranslateable Torinese exclamation. In the early days Ferruccio himself took a keen interest, and handing over his own car to two journalists for an early road test, explained the functioning of the controls, then opened the bonnet to expose 12 cylinders and six carburetters and said: 'Here as you see is just a simple engine.'

In performance the Countach approaches the ultimate Ferrari, the Berlinetta Boxer with the flat twelve engine derived from the racing car, but is not as refined although it is purely a road car without the Ferrari's racing ancestry.

The third member of the Modena trio, Maserati, also fell into the clutches of a commercial giant, the Citroën concern, even before oil prices spelt doom to fast cars. It is also the oldest of them all, the Maserati brothers fielding their first racer in 1926 in the Targa Florio round Sicily, a race invented by a local nobleman who wanted some fun.

Maserati had a longer and even more intensive racing history than Ferrari. They began in 1914 when Officina Alfieri Maserati opened in Bologna, Northern Italy, where perhaps the proximity of the Alps stimulates motoring competition. The trident of Neptune became the firm's badge, as it was the insignia of their town. They raced other people's cars, mainly Diattos, until their 1926 expedition to the Targa, where their new Maserati won the $1\frac{1}{2}$ litre class in its first race driven by Alfieri Maserati. The cars went on to be effective in Grand Prix racing until 1958 and sports car racing until 1964. Although the name had lived on, the three surviving Maserati brothers in the business had been taken over by the Orsi family in 1938. They were one of the few European makes to win at Indianapolis, in 1939 and 1940 with their 8-cylinder 3-litre supercharged 8CTF.

The sports car dynasty did not begin until 1946, when the six-cylinder sohc A6G appeared in 1·5- and 2-litre form. By then the firm had made its move (1941) from Bologna to Modena to become neighbours of Ferrari. The first for-sale road cars did not come until 1957 in the shape of the 3500GT, followed by the never-popular Quattroporte, then the 5000GT and the two-seater Mistrale coupe. Later the Mistrale and Sebring went up to four litres, and these are the road-going Masers, as opposed to the sports-racers, which are best remembered.

Later and more modern versions sported the four-cam V8 as

Where sports cars are mentioned there must be Ferraris. The 225 (*opposite, top*) was a development of the car which won the first post-war Le Mans race, has a 2.7-litre V12 engine. The Dino 246 (*above*) which has a firm place in the hall of fame, was named after Enzo Ferrari's only son, who died young, and is more highly-regarded by enthusiasts than its successor, the 308 (shown in its 1976 308GTB form, *opposite, below*)

in the Ghibli (hot wind), but they were a new generation, followed by the Indy (after the Citroën 1968 take-over), the Bora, the Khamsin with five litres (an even hotter wind) and the V6-engined Merak. In the case of Maserati the gulf between the road runners and the racers is even wider than their Modena neighbours, and in spite of their one-time dominance in racing the sports cars have never been big sellers or had quite the mystique of their two cousins, even if they look as beautiful and go as well, as their protagonists say. The racing 250F is still the yardstick by which others of the day are judged, and an engine from one of these powered the A6GCS in which Stirling Moss tackled the Mille Miglia. Moss drove 67 races in Masers of one kind and another, but was not too pleased when his brake pedal snapped off soon after the start of one Mille Miglia. In the case of some of the sports car models only ten or twelve examples were made, for instance the first series A6GCS and the flared-wing version with Carraroli coachwork. There were production models before the 1957 date quoted, but they were mostly for sale to amateur racing drivers, and in small series. In contrast 2 000 of the 3500GT were built. The most famous Maser of all, the 'birdcage', was the Tipo 60, a four-cylinder successful in sports-car racing. Only six were made in 1959–60, and much raced by Camoradi.

By the late 1960s sports car racing had come a long way from the 'road car' concept which governed events such as the Le Mans 24-hour race before the war. These three McLarens, driven by Chris Amon, Bruce McLaren and Denny Hulme at Laguna Seca in 1969, have the outrageous aerofoils which were seen in road racing for only a very short period. McLaren cars dominated the CanAm sports-racing championship for several years

In Britain the Jaguar C and D types and a few Aston Martins qualify under the hairy sports-racer banner, although the Ford GT40 and the Lola were also British-built, if some of their major components came from elsewhere. Most of the racing or near-racing machinery tends to be international in background as one firm gains dominance in the manufacture of one component, be it engine or shock absorbers, and becomes 'the' thing to have in order to win. Examples are legion in the history of the sport, but Cosworth, Coventry-Climax, and Bilstein spring to mind.

Jaguars C and D were close cousins, and unhappily the road-going version the XKSS came to a sudden end when only 18 had been made and the factory caught fire. But in its day (1957), the D-type so-called production model was rated the fastest car ever tested by the US journal *Road & Track*, with 162 mph top speed against a 2·9-litre Ferrari's 135 mph, and zero to 60 mph in 4·7 seconds. The D-type was of course a racing car constructed to win the Le Mans 24-hour race, which it did convincingly three times in four years, and the XKSS was an attempt to offer the closest thing to a sports-racer for sale to the public, an intention frustrated by the factory fire.

The D-type was a development of the earlier C-type, both of them good for more than 170 miles an hour in the 1950s, when few cars could come near this figure. It was based on the XK120 sports car, but obviously did not conform exactly to the road-going model which was in itself way ahead of the opposition in performance, if rather lacking in brakes. Main difference was that the C-type had a space-frame and the D-type used a mono-coque, whereas the 120 was built onto a chassis. Engine power was up by nearly 100 bhp from 150 to 245, which suggests a few internal differences.

Few Cs or Ds can have been driven very much on the public roads, but they were the ultimate tool in their day and long after.

Aston Martin come into our story with one or two of their models, the bulk of which have been for years fast, luxurious closed cars which do not fit into the road-burner category although they have big powerful engines and high top speed. It is the image of the businessman's express, a title used by the rival firm of Bristol, rather than the young man's dream car. But two models, the DBR and the Zagato, stir the blood a little more.

No beauty was the Allard, which followed the formula of a big American V8 engine in a home-made chassis with rather strange-shaped bodywork, functional rather than handsome

top
Jaguar's C-Type could be
driven on the road but was
really meant to be driven in
anger on the circuit, even if
nominally a two-seater sports
car. This is the winning car
at Le Mans in 1951

above
Aston Martin gained quite a
reputation with devices
like this 1934 Ulster, running
in the 1937 Le Mans 24-hour
race, and only moved on to
the lush closed commuting
types much later

above, right
This Aston DBR1 shot at
Lavant corner at Goodwood
two decades later makes an
interesting contrast and shows
development on the way
between sport-racer and
motor-way carriage

Aston began back in 1921, making before the war very pretty
but rather heavy and slow open cars which felt every matchstick
in the road. They progressed through various owners and crises
from the post-war DB2, with a 2·6-litre twin ohc Bentley-designed
engine, to the much larger 5·34-litre V8 introduced during the
1970s. The DBR won the Le Mans 24-hour race in 1959, and the
sports car constructors championship too, and fits into the image
of the wind-in-the-hair machine, as an open two-seater developed
from the DB3 and DB3S, which were factory-run prototypes.
This one had a five-speed box, not so common in 1956, a 230 bhp
dry sump engine, de Dion rear end, and disc brakes; its Le Mans
win was Aston's swan song in competition, apart from sporadic
attempts with prototypes.

The other machine which interests the sports-car man, the
DB4GT Zagato, followed the DBR in 1959 with the engine up
from three litres to four in a light-alloy block. Fewer than 20
were made, with 273 horse power, a 35-UK gallon tank stealing
all the luggage space, and spartan trim, allied to lighter weight.
It could top 150 mph and cover a standing quarter in 15 seconds.
This was the one to beat.

Our disguised racer, the Ford GT40, belongs to a different
family but must be the ultimate if performance is all and creature
comforts for the birds, who would need to be brave to come with
us. The GT40, which like the Jaguar Cs and Ds was built above

all to win at Le Mans, must be the most expensive winner ever, as Ford sent armies of men and machinery over in an abortive effort to beat Ferrari until he found the right formula to beat the Europeans at their own game. Earlier, the American company had even tried to buy Ferrari as a recipe for instant success, but this did not go through.

Finally their million-dollar investment brought four wins in a row in 1966–69, still not good enough to beat Ferrari's nine wins but up with Alfa and Jaguar and one behind Bentley. Curiously the first Le Mans cars were largely designed by Eric Broadley, based on his 1963 Lola, but these failed to win in 1964 or 1965. Then the 4·7-litre V8 grew to seven litres in new cars, and we once again saw proof that there is no substitute for cubic inches. The big bangers gave 530 bhp against the 450 of the best of the little 'uns.

Veteran race manager John Wyer built the original GT40s for Ford at his English workshop, went on building them, raced them after Ford had 'retired', and won Le Mans with them in 1968–69. Only 31 road-going GT40s were ever built as such, although a few racing cars have since been converted, so they remain exclusive at £5 900 plus tax. The road machine was pussyfooted down to 3·6 litres and 335 bhp, but still gave 164 mph in top gear or 142 in fourth. It must be the ultimate road car.

Eric Broadley of Lola sold more racing cars in his productive years than anyone else. He started with small cars but set himself to make the fastest Formula One car for the Bowmaker-Yeoman Credit racing team in 1962. They did not make it, and the cars went to other homes. Broadley then started using the 4·2 Ford V8 in a sports car, and he was almost home and dry. The first one appeared as the Mark 6 Lola GT at the British Racing Car Show of 1963. This was when Ford asked him to produce a Le Mans car which resulted in the GT40.

But Broadley did not hit it off with Ford and moved on, switching to the GM Chevrolet V8 unit for his next car, the racer T70. A bewildering number of racing types and models followed, but Broadley never made a road car. However, the Swiss designer Sbarro made a road-going Lola from the racer, together with the road-going conversion of a Porsche 917, this must be the original streetcar named desire.

Although French hopes for the Matra Grand Prix team were never fulfilled, the MS670 sports car derivative dominated that category of racing in the early 1970s

Modern Classics

Lovely cars which are a joy to behold and in some cases to drive too (never mind the others) give unalloyed pleasure to those lucky enough to be able to canalize their own taste and say 'This is what *I* want, forsaking all other'. Those who are rich enough can go one better and have a mixed stable of varying types of lovable car; the unhappy ones are those who love 'em all and cannot make their minds up which one to have an affair with, so spend their lives buying and selling and furbishing and regretting, and never achieving nirvana.

Cars from the past have been classified by various bodies who do not always agree as to what is what. In England the admitted authority is the Vintage Sports Car Club who say that Edwardian cars are those made before 31 December 1918; Vintage cars are those made up to 31 December 1930; Post-Vintage Cars are those made before 31 December 1940, but only certain Thoroughbreds listed in the Post-Vintage Thoroughbred List are eligible; and Historic Cars – which are all racers – were made between 1 January 1941 and 31 December 1960.

The agreed international classifications published by the F.I.V.A. (Fédération Internationale des Voiturettes Anciennes), representing 30 motoring clubs throughout the world, have a different dating list, and the Americans very sensibly lump them all together as Classics, which makes life easier. But when we come to cars which are neither Veteran (catered for by a different club, the Veteran Car Club) nor Vintage nor Historic, but which we think are nice and worth preserving, driving and drooling over there is no authority to say that our taste and judgment are correct and the one we have chosen is a true Classic and not just a dreadful mistake. There are dozens of one-make clubs and all sorts of other bodies, and the magazine *Thoroughbred and Classic Cars* used to list 38 makes of which they considered 81 models worth quoting every month so that would-be buyers could see how much they were likely to have to pay. However, dealers did not like this much as they considered the values were all too low, and the magazine has now dropped the list. We cannot consider 81 models in detail, even if we agree that they are all desirable, so the only way is to pick our own favourites among those cars which future generations are likely to say were worthwhile in their day and worth keeping.

Working alphabetically the first to come to us is AC, always a small producer and in recent years concentrated on models with a big American engine in a home-made chassis. This is a common formula employed by many others over the years, and

whether the result is worth preserving is an open question, the 428 and the Cobra are the ones to choose for those who care for that sort of thing.

Allard did much the same thing years earlier and in a cruder way. The only one of theirs we would nominate is the Cadillac-Allard, a sort of four-wheeled motor cycle with enormous straight-line performance. At least it's different. Alfa Romeo produced one of the prettiest cars of all time in their Giulietta coupe known as the Veloce in closed form or Sprint in spider shape, and some of these should certainly be put in the cupboard for posterity if we can find rust-free examples. The Giulietta came in 1954 with 1300 cc and could be Berlina, Sprint, Super, Sprint GT, Spider Veloce, so there is a wide choice, from Pininfarina, Bertone, and Zagato as well. It went on until 1962 when big brother Giulia took over with five speeds, 1570 cc and disc brakes. Like all Alfas it had a twin ohc engine.

Armstrong Siddeley must rate a place although it was a kind of down-market Daimler made for the chauffeur-driven trade. Somehow, the company missed this target; their last models the Sapphire and Star Sapphire were their best, big luxury limousines with all the 'wedding trimmings'.

Aston Martin we have talked about elsewhere and would again nominate the Zagato-bodies DB4GT and the DBR as the ones to seek and keep. Alvis probably made better cars before the war than after, and are no longer with us. The Old Grey Lady, especially in drophead form, had a classic line which seems to be missing from the later models. It belongs to the 1950s. Austin-Healey causes 'oohs' and 'aahs' from the young, but the big 3000 rally car had no ground clearance and was intolerably hot in the cockpit. Perhaps it is worth saving sentimentality for what it did in international rallies rather than for what it is, a memorial to brute force in engineering like the Allard.

Bentley is like Roquefort, either you are a blue cheese man or not. The post-war ones do not have great merit but are big and stately and if you want a Mark IV, R or S-Type help yourself. We would except the R-type Continental which had virtues of its own, although it was bulbous in appearance and not as handsome as some of the pre-war cars.

Bristol is a small producer whose cars got bigger and bigger from two litres up to six-and-a-half in the end, and are also an acquired taste. They were well, and expensively, made but with an American engine. Our taste runs to the early 400 and 401, which may be considered eccentric, but they were the best-looking of all the range, which grew fat and ugly with the passage of time, like some people.

BMW hit the mark before the war and did little after until the recent cars came along. Their V8 500 series models are listed as merit-worthy by some people but not by the authorities. The Daimler Dart which creeps into some lists of Desirables is a nasty-looking plastic monstrosity which gave endless trouble and is definitely out of court. Fiat's 2300s coupe made a habit of ringing bells when the handbrake was on or the choke out, but can be forgiven these musical habits if a rust-free one can be found. Some like the 124 Sport also. Both are from the 1965–67 era. The more modern 130 Coupe is a better bet.

Facel Vega was an odd French confection, again of the big American engine given better handling and brakes, but it did not sell very well, is ugly and less desirable than many other offerings. The little one with the Volvo engine, the Facellia, is even worse. Farrari. Ah, Ferrari. Some early ones were weird, but any of the later models will turn on any well-balanced male, right up to the five-litre Superfast, the biggest and bestest with all those cylinders and cams. Others may imitate but Chippendale and Ferrari set the standards by which others fail, and if that is partisan so be it. They must be painted blood-red and not over-silenced and if you cannot afford the petrol for them, then sell your wife or your home while you are young enough to enjoy the sound and fury at least once in your life. There is the

above
First Bristols had engines closely based on the famous BMW six-cylinder unit, but in 1962 the company turned to Chrysler for larger V8s. This is the two-litre 401 which was introduced in 1948

opposite
Fiat's XI/9 coupe has made its mark as a classic of the 1970s. It is seen here in the Dolomites in company with a Fiat 124 Abarth Rally

below
And what might THIS be? It is one of the last Bugattis of 1940, clad in a very English-looking body obviously parked in an English square, and must be a Type 57

The Ferrari Monza stood alone with a 160 mph top speed from its 3-litre engine in fifth gear. This one dates from 1954

opposite, top
Gordon-Keeble made one of the many fibreglass-bodied cars with American engines which graced the post-war scene. They are no longer with us but their cars have an increasing value

opposite, below
Aston Martin's DB series have improved over the years, with bigger engines, since they began in 1950

poor man's Ferrari, the Dino 246, which was a very nice car although it does have steel, aluminium and fibre-glass all mixed up at the front and hard to repair, but it will do if you cannot have the real thing. Some people think it an ugly thing with all those conflicting curves, others rave about its beauty.

Ford. Well, we have discussed the GT40 but the rest should be silence. Some people like Thunderbirds and Mustangs, but some like plastic tablecloths too. Do not join them. Frazer-Nash. Well, there are very few about but the Mille Miglia and Sebring and Le Mans replica are all desirable and beautiful and different and hard to find and enjoyable. You can tell the post-war models as they are the ones without chain drive.

Gordon-Keeble was another plastic car which had different names at different times, but was the old formula of a big American (Chevrolet) V8 engine in the maker's own chassis in fibre-glass clothing. It had good performance and handling and has a rarity value if you like that sort of thing. Healey, not to be confused with Austin-Healey, although both came from Donald Healey, produced an open two-seater around 1949 known as the Silverstone which looked pleasant in a functional way, and other Riley-engined models with various saloon and drophead bodies. They are also rare and handsome, and worth keeping.

HRG just about survived the war, although the open two-seater is very Vintage in concept with minimal concessions to comfort. They fetch more money than when new, but with a small engine (various types were used) are economical and about on a par with a Morgan in nostalgia time.

top
Iso Fidia was an Italo-American concoction conceived on the same lines as the Gordon-Keeble, using a Chevrolet V8, but Iso never achieved the status of the 'pure' Italian marques

above
Jokers may call this the revolting Iso but the Iso Rivolta A3 Lusso Grifo of 1964 with Bertone body looks businesslike and goes well even if the exhaust pipes are a bad joke

Iso made the Rivolta, the Fidia, Grifo and Lele to the familiar formula of a Chevrolet V8 in a made-up chassis with Italian coachwork clothing it. Renzo Rivolta had made money out of mopeds and thought he could undersell Ferrari *et al* in the fast luxury car market with a proper four-seater. The first Iso chassis was curiously like the Gordon-Keeble mentioned earlier. Bertone did the body, in 1962, and it was inevitably known jokingly as the revolting Iso. Are they worth keeping? They are high performance good-looking cars, fairly rare, but like so many others.

Jaguar must be mentioned, although they have been discussed in other chapters. Collectors go for the XK120 roadster rather than the later 140 and 150, and even the early E-types. They certainly have both the go and the looks, spares can be had, and were a motoring landmark, so the answer must be Yes to Jaguar as a classic. Things like the rare Mark V drophead are now sought after, and the lightweight aluminium-bodied XK120 is also a gem to look for. The swollen-bellied Mark 7, 8, 9 and 10 are even creeping back in some circles, although there are not too many wholesome examples around.

Jensen have gone the way of all good things after a bitter struggle, and people who have long been collecting the earlier CV8 and 541 models will no doubt want to add the final model, the Interceptor, to their collection. This again uses a big Ameri-

left
Alfa Romeo's lovely 6C Sport
with Zagato body stands for all
time as a classic in all
company, even if the 17/50 is
more fiery and dramatic and
better known

below
Buick's V8 open tourer, the
Roadmaster, has lines
familiar to film goers, and is
valued in the USA as one
worth keeping

Jaguar's Mark V drophead coupe was built in small numbers and is a rare and beautiful beast nowadays. It dates from 1949

can V8, in this case the Chrysler police car 7·2-litre motor, mounted in a reasonable chassis, with Italian clothing. It is quiet and civilized and powerful and if you can buy the fuel, well why not? Jowett is a name which has come up before, and the Javelin was worthy and the Jupiter different, if they both lacked a certain charm. There is a club for owners and they seek them out to restore, but it is not to everybody's taste.

Lagonda left us long ago, but the name came back on a four-door Aston Martin at the 1974 London Motor Show. Their first post-war car, the 2·5-litre in saloon and drophead coupe forms was criticized for complications like inboard disc brakes and did not exactly sell like hot cakes. As a result it is undervalued and the models of around 1950 can be bought for reasonable prices. They shared the Aston Martin engine, had good lines, and it is hard to understand why they are unloved, but a nice one would be worth cherishing. Lancia is a name for any car buff to conjure with, although they have been accused of always doing everything the hard way and building in complication for complexity's sake. There have been many models, but the Aurelia of 1950 onwards, the open two-seater B24GT, and the Flaminia of the 1960s must be classics. With their narrow V engines and handsome bodies and clever engineering the Lancias must be an investment, although not highly-priced at present.

Lea-Francis did not make much of a post-war splash, but their 14 Sports two-seater of around 1947 was one of the best looking cars of all time. Later, in 1950, came a four-cylinder 2·5-litre version of basically similar shape before the company went to the wall. This must rank as a classic in its own right and because of the company's pre-war engineering record with so many splendid devices which made all the right noises, some even supercharged. The Hyper was the one to own then.

Lotus is a very modern name to think of as a classic, but their first proper production model after the build-it-yourself open Seven was the Elite of around 1960, which offered handling and roadholding of a new order allied to tremendous performance from such a small (1216 cc) Coventry Climax engine. Fewer than 1 000 examples were made and the car has been called a commercial disaster for Lotus, as they lost money on each one, but it looked lovely, went well, and the problems of it all falling apart were eventually solved. Some of the later models may be better motor cars, but the Elite is the collectors' item of the range. The funny lift-out windows were a bit of a nuisance, but it was too noisy anyway with them in place.

Marcos is another make no longer with us, and perhaps in some

ways in the Lotus mould, a glass-fibre bodied 'special' mounted
on a made-up chassis with a bought-in engine. The Elite differed
in using the bodyshell as a chassis with the mechanical bits
bolted on, but Jem Marsh's Marcos had a frame underneath. He
made various models using MG, Volvo or Ford engines, and
they all looked marvellous and put the driver in a reclining
position in a hammock, which made vision a little difficult,
particularly in the wet if misting-up came on. Jem was a wild
enthusiast who managed to put his dreams into metal (or glass-
fibre) but there were certain impracticalities like a wooden
chassis, which provoked the usual crop of jokes about wood-
worm and the death-watch beetle. It was possible for wood
screws to fall out and affect things like the steering, but after all

Mosquito bombers were made of wood too. Few cars have been more unusual and just right for the man who wants something different.

Maserati comes next and could hardly be a more different kind of machine than the Marcos. We have already gone into their history, and some of the models, but in general most of them are not wildly sought-after and can be bought at reasonable prices. This excludes of course the racers like the 250F and refers to the more recent production cars. Perhaps the fact that the original company is in other hands affects the spares position, or the fact that people think it will put would-be owners off. Most Masers are handsome, and only the Quattroporte is regarded as something of an outsider. Go back as far as 1963 for the original production job, the 3500GT, or come closer today with a Mistrale, Sebring, Bora, Khamsin, Merak or Ghibli and they must be an ultimate investment.

Mercedes is a hard cat to classify, as the collectors' items are the pre-war monsters and the post-war ones a little too bread-and-butter to turn on the motoring nut. Exceptions are the 300SL, a brutal breath-taker which calls for some driving skill to tame, and the smaller and so-different 190SL, which did not offer much performance and had handling deficiencies, but was quite pretty. Some list the 230SL of about 1955, but there are not too many about. The 300SL is a very rare bird and expensive but obviously the one to go for if Mercedes is your thing, and you are not too poor.

opposite, top
The cars that no enthusiast could love: the European Safety Vehicles. These two are a Marina SRV2 and a Mercedes ESF 22 (white) produced to meet the regulations against bangs in the front, side, or elsewhere

opposite, lower
Porsche's 911 is the one all the young men want, but they may find it difficult to arrange insurance . . .

above
No-one has mass-produced a nicer shape than Jaguar's XK120, except perhaps Alfa with their Bertone model on the Giulia

Porsche's name makes the young hold their breath, but they have come a long way since this over-steering monster of a prototype for the original 356 crept on the scene in 1948

MG is a bit of a comedown from Mercedes and not what everyone would call a classic car, but the little two-seater T-series cars seem to have sold themselves to American students and become the thing to have on the campus, resulting in greatly inflated values for what is a somewhat ordinary mass-produced machine of no great performance, handling or roadholding and absolutely no luggage space. Their value must be in pure nostalgia for things gone as modern safety rules push the open car out of court. They are probably as good for the liver as horse riding and do not use as much hay. The earlier the suffix the better, i.e. a TA is better than a TF from a value viewpoint, although the TF is a better car with some suspension and other improvements. For the trendy young man rather than those who care about cars.

Morgan looks like MG but is even more old-fashioned, apart from the later V8-engined ones which really GO. They have kept the same design for longer than anyone can remember, but that seems to be the way people like it and they are crying all the way to the bank. There is nowhere to put your toothbrush and you leap from crest to crest of the road bumps while sitting low enough to scrape your knuckles on the road. It is a strange form of masochism which makes people pay for their own torture, but there are enough about to keep the firm healthy since 1910, when their cars had only three wheels. It does not much matter which model you choose, as they are much alike.

Porsche means magic to the fast car lover, and the firm have come a long way since oversteer was another word for Porsche. Some people are saving the rather curvaceous early 356s, but for a car to use the later 911 series is infinitely better, and the later the model the better in terms of just about everything, including curiously enough fuel consumption which improved as the engines got bigger and bigger from two litres to 2·4 to 2·7. The shape has not changed much over the years, air cooling means some noise, but the Porsche brings driving joys of its own which are unmatched by other makes.

Reliant make more three-wheelers and small (850 cc) cars than anything else, but their Scimitar GTE has gained classic status, and the earlier saloon is also respected. Bodies are glassfibre so non-rusting, and mechanical bits are Ford so no problem. They are also nice people to deal with, which endears a man to his car maker. A Scimitar saloon or a latter GTE would make sense to keep as the product of one of our more individual manufacturers.

Riley is an honoured name which ceased to mean a different and individual motor car a few years ago when it became an Austin/Morris with a Riley badge. We had for example the Pathfinder, which was an amalgam of bits and pieces, and the last Rileys in their own right were the 1·5 and 2·5 saloons of 1946 to 1953, of which there were also drophead coupe and open versions. These were well made if heavy cars, with a restricted steering lock in the case of the bigger 2·5-litre model. The smaller one was a bit pushed to cope with all the weight, and people tried twin carburetters to help. The open three-seater 2·5 is un-

top
Reliant's Scimitar GTE has grown up into a wider, longer shape since the first Ford-engined model and has a big following

above
Lotus is too young to be a modern classic, but must join the immortals eventually with the 1974 Elite, which pushed the company into a higher price-bracket market

Rolls-Royce looked much nicer before the war when different coachbuilders clad them. This elegant Wraith of 1939 graces a stand at the Berlin show with a very continental air

fortunately hideously ugly, but there is a better-looking drophead. The saloons with torsion-bar suspension and the trend-setting vinyl-covered roofs were well-proportioned, and do not command big prices for those who think they are worth keeping.

Rolls-Royce is more than a motor car to most people, and is perhaps the ultimate public relations exercise, as only a miniscule fraction of all those people who think they are wonderful have ever ridden in one to test their preformed impressions. Everyone knows the old tag about the triumph of workmanship over design, and certainly they have always been rather old-fashioned cars. But as everyone's mind is made up there is not much point in talking about them, except to say that the one to keep in the post-war range seems to be the Silver Dawn This is a Mark VI Bentley with a RR radiator, but for reasons unknown it is highly valued.

Sunbeam in its post-war form we would not include, save perhaps for the Tiger, an American V8-engined special which had many faults like wind noise, overheating in the cockpit and many worse. But not many were made and it is better than those Alpines and things.

Triumph. Well, we feel much the same about them. The TRs are another and rougher kind of MG of an agricultural nature. There was the open thing called the 1800 or Roadster which had peculiarity value, and is collected by some fanatics, although it did not go particularly well or look very nice.

TVR is a funny British plastic car which has survived all the vicissitudes of the years and is still in business with Ford engines now. It has a high scuttle which dates it but the fans are queueing up to buy old ones because they do not make enough new ones, like Morgan. It is all sorted now and civilized, and you might do worse than try one, although plastic classics seem a bit suspect.

Sport becomes Entertainment

Motor racing began in 1895 in France as a rarified form of sport for the wealthy few, but it is hard to determine exactly when it moved into the combination of industry and showbiz which it has undoubtedly become today. One could argue that this started very early with the Pekin–Paris 'race' of 1907 which was organized by a newspaper and certainly surrounded by ballyhoo in the best American tradition, but at the same time it was a very tough trial for people who knew what they were about, or at least thought they did until the true horrors of crossing some of the impossible and almost impassable terrain involved became apparent. The victor had to be a nobleman, Prince Scipione Borghese, driving an Itala, part of it on railway lines.

Racing began obviously on the public roads as there was nowhere else to go, but early in this century was driven away by accidents and public opposition onto closed circuits of roads or private tracks, where it has stayed ever since with one or two notable exceptions. The best-known and most used track was the first of them all, Brooklands in Surrey, England which opened in 1907, the same year curiously enough as the Pekin–Paris. Two years later came Indianapolis in the United States, whose fame rests on one annual event, the 500, which has gone on uninterrupted except by the two world wars of this century.

Indy has seating for more than 200 000 people, and the only other site which can rival this sort of attendance is the Sarthe circuit near Le Mans in France where the annual 24-hour race was first run in 1923; this has attracted crowds of up to a quarter of a million people, but long-distance sports-car racing faded away, and today's emasculated spectacle attracts perhaps half that number, although it is a traditional French holiday outing. The Sarthe circuit is made up of a network of public roads which are closed to traffic for the occasion, unlike the other two tracks which are entirely artificial for racing only.

Since 1972 Grand Prix racing, which is supposed to be the ultimate, has been run in a strange way. The builders of the racing cars, who have banded together as the Formula 1 Constructors Association, sell each of the 14 or so events each year which count towards the international championship to the organizers of the race, usually a motor club, as a package and then divide up the spoils between their members.

The going rate for a race-package is now about £170 000 rising to £190 000 in 1978, and although people involved in motor racing tend to be rather secretive about their finances it is not hard to work out that running a racing team can be a paying proposition.

The way it used to be. The Delage V12 two-litre racing car of 1925, finished in France's national blue

This has not always been so, as many have found out to their cost. The exception to the rule of secrecy comes in the case of the Americans, who like to tell everyone how much money they have and earn. The Indianapolis Motor Speedway publishes all the prizes in its annual programme of the race, and as long ago as 1970 had given away more than eight and a half million dollars, excluding the lap and accessory prize money, which would increase the total by a big percentage. They even list the names of all drivers and how much they have won each over the years, which would make a modern European Grand Prix driver, hiding away from the tax man in Switzerland, jump up and down in rage at the degree of indiscretion.

In the beginning, when races were run on public roads, people simply turned up to watch at the roadside and no-one could say them nay; it was all free, which broke the hearts of would-be promoters who quickly saw a chance to earn a more or less honest income from charging the public to see the gladiators. When the ill-fated Paris–Madrid race started from the gates of Paris there was such a mêlée of people and cyclists that it was a job to get the cars away at all, although it was at some ungodly hour in the morning when it was not expected that many people would be awake, and only the birds astir.

When competition moved onto enclosed circuits, it became much easier to collect the gate money. The Le Mans organizers, the Automobile Club de l'Ouest, showed sufficient financial acumen to fence in a large portion of Northern France as securely as Cape Cannaveral at launch time for the period of

A racer that could be driven on the road, or a road car that could be raced—Amilcar CGS of 1927

their fiesta, and charge people to take themselves, their transport and usually tent and/or caravan in as well. They did it so efficiently that sometimes competing drivers were hard put to it to reach their cars.

But the master of such situations was the inimitable M. Eugene Mauve, a French pilot during the First World War, who conceived the idea of running a race in the forest of St Germain outside Paris, a sort of woody common where the inhabitants were wont to take picnics and such on public holidays and weekends, and still are come to that. He persuaded the local authorities by undisclosed means to close the public roads for no less than 50 hours at Whitsun in 1922 for *two* 24-hour races, one for motor cycles and the other for light cars and cyclecars, with a two-hour interval in between. He called his races the *Bol d'Or*, although whatever substance the winner's trophy was made of it certainly was not gold. After presenting it each year he took it back again for the next event. The name still survives in the motor cycle world.

Cyclecars should perhaps be explained. They were sort of minimal, cheap-to-build and run vehicles, often with three wheels. One anonymous writer at the time described them: 'combining the comfort of a cement mixer, the noise of a pneumatic drill and the directional stability of a chicken with its head off'. There was one make, the Bédélia, on which the favourite joke of the day was to cross the steering wires so that turning the wheel produced the opposite result to that intended, with amusing results to the watchers.

But M. Mauve was a specialist, indeed *the* specialist in cyclecars, which he built himself. Fortunately they did not survive very long. In his race M. Mauve permitted only one driver per car, which means the poor fellow had to keep going for 24 hours, something of a job in such primitive machinery, but luckily most of them broke down or the wheels fell off after a short time. The patron formed the Association Auto-Motor-Cycle-Cariste

below
Enough to bring tears to the eyes. The Barnato and Birkin Bentley on its way to a 1929 win on the Le Mans circuit in the annual 24-hour race, which Bentley made a habit of winning

bottom
Ascari shows the way through the streets, with a rope to keep the people back, in a big banger Ferrari in 1950

de France (AAMCCF), in which he held all offices, to promote and run the events. Unlike today's drivers, who are paid for their services, those competing on the triangle of roads in the St Germain forest had to pay for the privilege. The boss could not charge the 75 000 or so watchers who trekked into the forest to see the races as they were on public land, but he made do by selling catering concessions which kept the wolf from his door. He paid no starting money, bonuses or prize money, so it was a profitable enterprise. He also built rather temporary 'grandstands' and sold seats.

Sydney Horstman built the cars which bore his name in Bath from 1914 to 1929, and they ran in many competitions. This 1921 ex-works Super Sports used a 1440 cc Anzani engine in its polished aluminium body

Moss on Mercedes passing the harbour in the modern street race round the houses of Monte Carlo on the old circuit, now changed to make the pit siting safer

above
How it has all changed. The Grand Prix is supposed to be the ultimate in motor racing, but it's not like this now. The great Farina driving an Alfa in the 1950 Italian GP when they didn't even wear crash helmets

After some trouble over casualties among the spectators the race moved to another forest, at Fontainebleau and then to a different kind of setting, the Montlhéry track near Paris, but things were never the same. M. Mauve had given someone ideas though, and the Le Mans 24-hour race began one year after his Bol d'Or decimated the roadside trees in the forest of St Germain. The ex-pilot is not a great figure in the history of motor sport, but an amusing one, and certainly one of the first to move the operation into the showbiz era.

But most of the pre-1939 racing was a rather private business for initiates, at which the cognoscenti gathered like Freemasons to go through their ceremonies, which were not considered of much interest to the public at large. The spectacles at Le Mans and Indianapolis were exceptions where the man-in-the-street was allowed in for an annual peep at his betters at play. This attitude was no secret at the Brooklands track, where the advertising posters—what few there were in selected spots—bore the legend: 'The right crowd and no crowding'. In the early days drivers wore jockeys' silks inherited from the turf, prizes were in guineas, and there were even bookmakers, who vanished from the scene until they came back to one or two circuits recently as a great innovation.

Most drivers were wealthy playboys typified by the so-called Bentley Boys of the 1920s, led by the diamond millionaire Woolf Barnato, given to wild parties between races. Earning a living was not one of the distractions which hampered their fun or wasted their gilded time. Some dallied with a little business. Captain Sir Malcolm Campbell, a typical wealthy playboy of the era, was in theory an insurance underwriter and is sometimes credited with inventing libel insurance for publishers, but that did not occupy too much of his working day. Brooklands, unlike the once-a-year tracks, was in daily use for testing, trying out modifications; tyres and every conceivable thing that could go wrong were hammered over the bumpy concrete. Montlhéry in France which opened later was a similar establishment, where the really keen mechanics and tuners lived on the premises.

Motor clubs organized the races, and made a good income from it, even if the gentleman-amateur drivers were spending their own gold. If 30 000 people attended a Brooklands meeting it was a big day. The origin of the place was that the builder and owner of the site, Hugh Lock King, MP, decided it was time that

British manufacturers had somewhere to test and develop their cars. So he built the track, at a cost of well over a million pounds in today's money, but never made a profit, although the Brooklands Automobile Racing Club which ran the races did. The track or what was left of it, as a large slice had been taken out of the banking to admit aircraft, was sold after the Second World War.

The showman element came into motor sport with a vengeance after that war when people were hungry for any kind of entertainment and excitement, and soon began to be able to afford it even if they had soon spent any money they gathered up on leaving the forces. The British Racing Drivers Club opened up a track on an old airfield at Silverstone, more or less in the middle of England and accessible to all, and down in Sussex the Duke of Richmond did the same thing with the old Westhampnett fighter field on his estate, Goodwood. Brooklands was gone but a

Outstanding Grand Prix combination of the early 1970s—Jackie Stewart in a Tyrrell (here at Monaco)

former grass track at Brands Hatch in Kent, only 20 miles from London was expanding and claiming the customers.

The *Daily Express* newspaper realized that motor sport could sell newspapers and backed the BRDC meetings at Silverstone, putting on any kind of stunt which would pull the customers in. The entertainment era was really with us. Drivers soon began to realise that they had crowd-pulling value and starting money came into the language. One of the first talented drivers to put his affairs on a proper business basis was Stirling Moss. Drivers are always a bit shy about how much money they make, but it was said that Stirling was taking home £75 000 a year when the pound was worth about three times what it is now. Contracts were signed with an oil company for fuel, a tyre company, a plug manufacturer and all kinds of other ancillary suppliers to make up the total in addition to fees from the car manufacturer, starting money, prize money, TV, radio and journalistic fees, promotion fees, sponsoring deals for custard or cornflakes, and so on.

As the world settled down to a peacetime economy again motor sport proliferated. At first fuel was scarce in some countries, and in Britain it was rationed for many years, but the races went on. Grand Prix racing was to a formula allowing engines of 1·5 litres supercharged or 4·5 unsupercharged, which came into force in 1948, and has subsequently been for cars with 2-litre unsupercharged engines (1952–53); 2½-litre engines (1954–60); 1½-litre engines (1961–65); and 3-litre engines from 1966.

Immediately before the war the state-backed German teams from Mercedes and Auto-Union had almost unlimited money at their disposal, but this was a different thing from the entertainment element of making a business out of racing by giving the public all the thrills and spills which could be contrived–or at least promising them something good. It was not unknown for the participation of star drivers to be promised when there was not a cat in Hell's chance that they would be there. . . .

left
Jack Brabham, the only driver to build his own car and win the championship, sliding round Stowe in the 1966 Silverstone International Trophy

below
After an 11-year interval, Ferrari gained world championship honours in 1975, when Austrian Niki Lauda won the drivers' title. He was runner up in 1976 in the sleek 12-cylinder Ferrari (here in the Monaco GP)

Circuit owners and organizing clubs had nobody to represent them collectively, and negotiated individually with works teams or with drivers, although each one had a reasonably accurate idea of what the other was paying, in spite of the inevitable poker game played by both sides in an effort to up (or down) the ante. Life was much simpler for organizers though before the invention of Armco, catch netting, run-off areas and all the rest of the modern safety devices. Their main problem was to get the drivers, who would play hard-to-get when races clashed, as they could before all the organizing machinery of the Federation Internationale de l'Automobile rumbled into action from the Place de la Concorde where its International Sporting Commission (CSI) lurked. This body is traditionally made up of very old gentlemen who might have managed the Paris–Madrid very well but tend to be out of touch with the sport in the second half of the 20th century. Their one concession to modernity has been to change their name in post-war days from the even more unwieldy old one of Association Internationale des Automobile Club Reconnus (AIACR). They will remember, even if most people still alive have forgotten, that in fact the first motor competition of all, the 90-mile Paris–Rouen of 1894, was in fact sponsored by a newspaper, the *Petit Journal*.

In the sacred name of publicity, oil and tyre companies and others once handed out largesse in the form of goods or money in the way of bonuses to competitors even in quite minor club events. That has all largely gone by the board in the wake of the economic crisis and the changing attitude of sponsors. There has been some switch from racing to rallying, which some big companies now feel attracts more public notice, but as has been pointed out the first time a rally car goes into the badly-sited and uncontrolled spectators and causes casualties that will be the end of the sport which is now so booming, as governments react as they did after the big Le Mans disaster in 1955 when 80 people died. There has been no motor racing in Switzerland since, although the holocaust happened in France.

'Yumping' is a self-explanatory Scandinavian term; the action is demonstrated here in an Opel by the Finnish driver Ari Vatanen

Although drivers and others in Grand Prix racing are fond of publishing their memoirs we never learn much about the financial side of things, or the other behind-the-scenes activities which might be of interest. An exception is Rob Walker, who was a long-time entrant of cars in GP races; he revealed in 1969 that BP had been supporting him to the tune of 25 000 dollars a year until they, along with most other major oil companies, decided that the racing game was not worth the candle. He also said that Firestone gave him free tyres, plus servicing and a 'generous contract', and that Autolite plugs, Girling brakes and Ferodo linings all chipped in with some cash or material, while he had support to a total of 12 500 dollars a year from Heuer watches (his driver, Jo Siffert, was Swiss), Hart Skis, Bio-Strath Health Tonic and Vibrometer instruments. At that time he said a car with a spare engine cost 60 000 dollars and to run a team like BRM cost 750 000 dollars a year and a one-car team like his own 150 000 dollars annually.

So much for one man's figures a few years back, but the whole scene has changed since then with the drivers forming their trade union, which now seems to have fallen apart, the circuit owners banding together, and the car makers very much in control with their package-race deal with the race organizers. In addition to their global sum to put a race on, the transport of

top
The Lotus Grand Prix team started a trend by painting their 49s in the colours of a cigarette brand, and then went the whole way with their 72s, which were dubbed 'John Player Specials'. Here Brazilian Emerson Fittipaldi drives his JPS towards victory in the 1972 British Grand Prix, the year when he first won the world championship

above
Indianapolis turning point came in 1965, when Jim Clark won the race at over 150 mph, for the first time in its history. Clark drove a rear-engined Lotus-Ford, and completely dominated a field largely made up of traditional front-engined USAC 'roadsters'

BMW made great efforts to win the European Touring Car Championship in the early 1970s, when their sternest opposition came from Ford, and in 1976 they raced outwardly similar cars in the new World Championship of Makes. Here a 'normal' 3.4-litre BMW is passed by the then-new turbocharged version (nearest camera) at Silverstone in 1976

their cars, drivers, mechanics and team hangers-on is paid for by the race organizers if the event is outside Europe. This could add, say, £90 000 if the race were as far away as South Africa or South America.

The French Elf oil company, which unlike BP and some others is still in the sponsoring business, say they put £40 000 into each race to keep Ken Tyrell's six-wheelers going. Cigarette companies have flirted with motor racing, some, like John Player, remaining constant in their support of Lotus for several seasons. In 1976 the ten Formula 1 teams who are members of the Constructors Association shared about two million pounds or a little more in package payments for 14 major races, but money they receive from other sources like sponsors would more than double this. On Rob Walker's figures, even without allowing for the increase in costs and the decrease in the value of money since then, they would not even break even, which people in the business find it hard to believe. It all depends upon whose figures you believe.

On the other side of the fence, race organizers claim that it can cost up to £250 000 to stage a major event like a Grand Prix, and they are constantly spending money on capital investments to meet the demands for more and more safety measures. Examples are the new pits and chicane at Silverstone, and a completely revamped circuit at Brands Hatch. In Europe some long established tracks like Spa-Francorchamps and others have gone out of use as 'unsafe' after decades of use by less demanding pilots.

left
Martini, Fina, Goodyear join
in the mobile hoarding of the
modern GP circus (the cars are
actually Brabhams in 1975).
Armco barriers also show this
is modern times

below
Last of the great road races,
still just surviving although no
longer acceptable as a
championship event, the Targa
Florio round the slippery
roads of Sicily was the one to
watch. Here is Redman in his
Porsche 908 winning the
1970 event, on his way
through Campofelice

We now have the tacit admission that motor racing is a business like any other and must show a profit or die, in spite of the dedicated efforts of some people like the racing mechanics who work night and day, presumably because they like it.

There has always been a close connection between motor racing and the publishing world, right since *Petit Journal* sponsored that first-ever race, and many journalists have dabbled in the lower reaches of the sport. In earlier times Sammy Davis, who was sports editor of *The Autocar*, was one of the Bentley Boys, although he had no money of his own, and was perhaps made welcome, driving ability apart, for what he could do for the team in the way of press coverage. Certainly the salary of a weekly journalist in the 1920s would not have run many Bentleys, or bicycles if it comes to that.

In later times his mantle fell on Dennis Jenkinson of *Motor Sport*, who made the famous Mille Miglia runs as navigator with Stirling Moss on Mercedes and was cool enough to keep a detailed log and write about it, and Paul Frere and Harald Erth who raced Grand Prix cars. There is also a keeness among race organizers now to recruit people like disc jockeys from radio and TV to drive in celebrity races, which begins to look like putting the cart before the horse, although some are talented enough to perform in their own right in minor events.

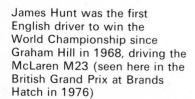

James Hunt was the first English driver to win the World Championship since Graham Hill in 1968, driving the McLaren M23 (seen here in the British Grand Prix at Brands Hatch in 1976)

If we see films of the heroic age of the early part of the Century it is obvious that much of the spectacle has gone out of the sport, although there may be some similarity between the sliding monsters of the early 1900s and the saloons on the forest special stages of modern rallies. These can still be watched without payment if you are keen enough and brave enough to stay up all night in the cold and wet of a forest to watch a few headlamps flash by.

As the natural spectacle has gone out as cars have become more stable and less dramatic so the showbiz element has come in to try to sell a declining show, like the circus without the elephants and the acrobats. The Formula I scene is now such a closed shop that it is more like a chess match played by tele-printer, so esoteric that few can understand, and far removed from the smoke-belching 'dicing with death' monsters which enlivened the early scene.

Modern Grand Prix fields vary little from race to race, as the 'Grand Prix circus' travels from circuit to circuit, and continent to continent. This group at the start of the 1975 German Grand Prix is typical with cars from the Brabham, Tyrell, McLaren, March, Ferrari, Lotus and Shadow teams prominent

Cars for the Few

This Métallurgique was one of the monster-engined cars of the early part of the century which is still driven on the roads today and is capable of well over 100 mph—if the driver is brave

opposite, top
Luxury from the past, and one that has not inspired a plastic copy yet. This 1928 Hispano-Suiza eight-litre Boulogne with body by Gurney Nutting shouts out its origins in the age of luxury and cheap labour

opposite, lower
The most expensive Rolls and one of the ugliest ever, the £30 000 Camargue, which spoils a long tradition of beautiful lines and luxury

The perversity of man has expressed itself as much through the motor car as in any other way; thus as soon as the car could be produced in large numbers and was reliable, rugged individualists wanted to reverse the pendulum, and as soon as they were able to have a car just like everyone else's model they wanted one that was entirely different and individual.

In the early days people mounted wicker armchairs on big chassis, and later put surplus aero engines into cars, all in the search for something different from what the man next door had. Once the car-coachbuilding industry was established a man could express his whims easily; all he needed was a cheque book, and some pretty bizarre creations came into being on the demand of some rich but misguided tycoons.

There were so many big chassis available in the 1920s and 1930s that there was ample scope for the special builder, as we might call him today. In England there were Bentley, Daimler and Rolls-Royce, to name the best known; in Europe, Minerva, Isotta-Fraschini, Hispano-Suiza, Delage, Delahaye, and in the United States an even greater number of outsize machines on which the body-builder could do his worst.

But once the number of manufacturers had been slimmed down by wars and economic factors and all the coachbuilders had gone, except for a few hardy Italians who are still in independent business, the task of the man who wanted Something Different had become much harder. Thus the custom car business has sprung up, mainly in the United States, in which stock models are painted in way-out and weird colours and patterns or even rebodied in a bid for individuality.

There has also been a rash of modern re-creations of old-time models which were famous in their day for their beauty or performance or a combination of the two. The brand-new Veteran or Vintage car brings only scorn from the died-in-the-wool lover of the real thing, who perhaps sees his investment threatened, but these spanking-new 'antiques' give people harmless fun and have the advantage over the real thing of such amenities as brakes, easy starting and reliability.

Many of the companies launched forth in a blaze of enthusiasm came to a sad end when still young, but two or three have made a successful business of bringing the past back to life. Perhaps the oldest-running and best known are the Stevens Brothers in Milwaukee, Wisconsin who traded originally as SS Automobiles Incorporated from 1735 South 106th Street.

The guiding hand and inspiration came from Brooks Stevens, who designed many bodies for special show models which appeared at the Paris, Geneva and Turin salons. Then in 1964 he produced at the New York show his Excalibur SS, which looked like a pre-war Mercedes SSK but was in fact Chevrolet Corvette bits mounted upon a Studebaker frame with a fake-Mercedes type body. The less said about the handling of this one the better, but it looked the part on the boulevard.

One year after the Series I came the Series II, which offered the mixture more or less as before plus the option of a three-speed Turbo-Hydramatic 400 automatic transmission and Corvette suspension. The slogan was to combine the dependability of today with the nostalgia of yesterday, or the comfort of the 1970s in a 1927 style. The SS company went on to offer a variety of models, the Excalibur SS Roadster, a two-seat cycle-wing monster with chromed flexible outside exhaust pipes, a similar model with long wings or fenders, and a Phaeton which was a four-seat version of the long-wing model. They claimed zero to 60 in six seconds and 150 miles an hour, but the top speed claim at least sounds dubious, with that far-from wind-cheating styling. They cost around 12 000 or 13 000 dollars in 1965, and several hundred were sold.

Eventually they ran out of surplus Studebaker chassis after Studebaker had closed down, and made up their own frame, which improved the handling. William C. Stevens, the vice-president and son of the designer, expected that the emission and safety laws would eventually put them out of business, but meanwhile they were making a lot of cars.

above
Another beauty from the same house. This Maybach cabriolet which looks remarkably sleek for such a big car, even if festooned in front in the Christmas-tree manner of the 1938–9 period

left
Replicars offer some of the looks of the beautiful oldsters allied to modern advantages like brakes and easy starting. This was an attempt at the classic 17/50 Zagato Alfa Romeo, inspired by the Italian magazine *Quattroroute*, and made of modern production components

below
Big could be Beautiful, as Delage showed on this D8 model of 1930 with double-cowl body rather in the American style

An off-shoot of the fake Mercedes which also came from Excalibur was the 35X Excalibur, one of several attempts to cash in on the immortal fame of the Type 35 Bugatti and produce something which looked like the original without its temperament. Their car was quite a passable imitation except that it was much wider and lower, but still offered room only for a toothbrush. It did have the advantage of the reliable mechanical bits of the Opel Commodore GS in place of Ettore Bugatti's eccentricities.

This one was offered by Guy Storr, who lived in Monaco but had the cars assembled in Moncalieri, Italy, and regularly produced one at the Geneva motor show for several years. It had a six-cylinder 2·5 litre engine producing 130 DIN horsepower and was claimed to do 200 km/h and the standing-start kilometre in 30 seconds, but whether any were ever made or sold is doubtful. It had modern conveniences like automatic transmission, was painted the traditional Bugatti French blue, and looked very pretty. It weighed 880 kilograms empty, and should have been one of the more successful of these new-for-old ventures.

A similar attempt at a fake Bugatti Type 35 was made by an English company which gave the car the odd name of the Dri-Sleeve, because they supplied a plastic arm-cover to keep the driver's right arm dry in this rather fresh-air kind of motoring. Not too many of those have been seen about either.

The other successful company in the bogus oldie business is Panther Westwinds Ltd, operating near the old Brooklands track in England, who started off with a similar venture to the Excalibur, except that in this case their car was a copy of the original Jaguar SS100, the Panther J72 and faithful to the original in that it did have a Jaguar engine. Later models went to the V12 as in the last E-Type Jaguar, and it had enormous straight-line performance. Other projects included something which looked like a Ferrari but wasn't, exhibited at Continental shows, and

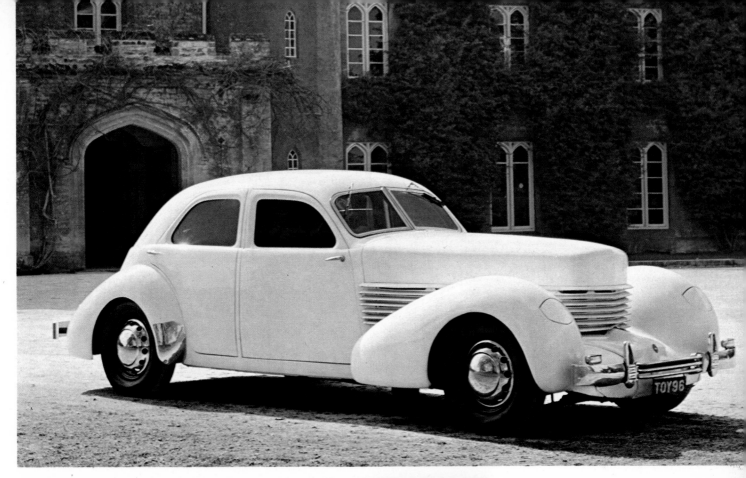

the final glory, a massive vehicle which looked like a Bugatti
Royale but wasn't.

This one, entitled the De Ville, cost £17 650 and was 204 inches
long and must be the ultimate rich man's folly. The Panther
company also do trimming work for other companies, so can use
their way out replicars as extravagent publicity aids for their
business, even if they do not sell too many.

The many other would-be golden oldies have included the
Alfa-Romeo Zagato 1750, which was also reasonably faithful to
the original pre-war and immortal 17/50 in appearance, but used
modern mass-produced Alfa bits. The Italian motoring magazine
Quattroroute had a hand in its conception, but once again it does
not appear to have been a big seller.

Another model which did not make it was the Ruger, a modern copy of the 4·5-litre Bentley tourer of the 1920s produced by an American gunsmith. There was also a three-quarter size revival of the pre-war US Classic the Cord, which we have not seen. Perhaps it would be better not to mention things like plastic Rolls-Royce fronts for fitting to Volkswagens or Chevrolets, according to taste or lack of it.

Other misguided efforts have included a device known as the Guyson E-type, which eliminates the beautiful lines of the E-type Jaguar and replaces them with squared-off tank-like angles. There are also several re-creations of the racing D-type Jaguars which cost more than the originals, if there were any originals left to be found.

In addition to the three-quarter sized Cord–strictly speaking it was eight-tenths size to accord with the model name of the original the Cord 810–Glenn Pray later offered a shrunken Auburn Speedster in 1967. At an auction run by the London fine art firm of Christie's in Geneva in 1976 an original Auburn, found in the traditional farmyard complete with chicken's feathers, fetched a top bid of £8 000, so perhaps they were worth copying.

Another US classic was revived in name only in a curious exercise which was presumably an attempt to cash in on the nostalgia value of the memorable Stutz Black Hawk. The modern version designed by former Chrysler stylist Virgil Exner was a contemporary saloon with an Italian-made body powered by Pontiac with hangover suggestions of the old shape in head-lamps, wings and grille. That probably made no-one rich.

M. Sbarro, who made the Lola streetcar mentioned earlier, produced one of the most practical combinations of fond memories allied to get-up-and-go in his current copy of the much-adored BMW 328 of pre-war fame. This looks pretty much like the original but has all-modern BMW parts, apart from the front suspension which is borrowed from a long-dead NSU model, the 1200. The buyer can choose his engine from the current BMW range, and the result probably goes better than the original spartan two-litre, and has factory warranty too. An original 328 with factory racing history changed hands recently for more than £10 000 and is now in the works museum at Munich.

Italy has produced two vehicles which are not replicars but in the same genre for the man who has everything and wants something different. Both were rear-engined and based on Fiat mechanicals, but dressed up with fake radiator grilles to look like 'normal' cars. One, the Siata 850, looked vaguely like an MG but had nasty touches like visible external door-hinges *à la Mini* and was hardly in the tradition of luxury Italian coachbuilding. It had wire wheels and a sort of sporty look. The companion model, the Vignale Gamine, was smaller and looked frailer, with more of the mobile shopping basket than the sports car about it. Both were more suited to sunny Italy or California than ruder climes.

In similar vein was the English SP Highwayman, which did not actually come to market. It was said to be a general exercise in copying the lines of the 1930s without any particular model in mind, but had the look of an Invicta which had been harshly treated by an unsympathetic owner. The engine would have been a Rover V8, based on the old Oldsmobile block. Another British Leyland cocktail, not offered by them but by an independent, was the Ziglair composed of Triumph chassis parts and an MG engine with a Riley Imp air about it.

All those mentioned have been attempts to recreate what might loosely be called Vintage cars, but there is one other curiosity made in England which is more in the Veteran or more specifically Edwardian theme. It is known as the Albany and is supposed to suggest a hint of 1904 Fiat or 1908 Opel, although the two-seater body is mounted on a box-section modern chassis powered by a Triumph Spitfire engine governed to 40 mph. It has wheels with what look like fat wooden cart-type spokes, but they are fake too, being in cast aluminium. This too is a fair-weather conveyance.

below
This 1973 Mustang Ghia from Ford shows what the US can do to the work of an Italian stylist if they try and pay enough. Let us shed Ghia tears

bottom
Italy always makes the pretty ones, and this Lancia B24 Aurelia spider shows a marvellous simplicity of line which has the touch of a master

Some of the strange vehicles made for use in films or for publicity purposes deserve a mention as sometimes the workmanship is of a very high standard, even though the 'Rolls-Royce' may turn out to be a Plymouth underneath the cardboard and the 1904 Veteran to have an invisible automatic transmission. Although these specimens are not normally made for sale some have been driven around the public roads to cause a sensation and do fit into the 'one-off' category.

In the field of the dream car or one-off prototype rather than the imitation throwback Italy still reigns supreme, although sometimes the same examples do pop up again year after year having shed their skins and acquired new ones. Unhappily many of the once proud and independent coachbuilding houses have been taken over by the car makers and are producing series runs rather than original designs which were once their forté. Since the supercar market was eliminated by the world energy crisis, the whole Italian scene has changed and the artists in metal are likely in future to be making bread-and-butter cars rather than the extravaganzas which used to be such a feature of the coachbuilders' section of the Turin show each year.

There are still cars like the Jaguar XJS, which can exceed 150 miles an hour and costs less than half the price of a Ferrari or Lamborghini, yet price is not really the criterion of the man in this market. How the wind of change is blowing is shown by the attitude of Porsche, who after starting with a car made from Volkswagen parts then moving over to a very expensive and individual machine have now gone full circle back to the mass-produced parts again with their 924. This car, cheaper by half than their 911S series, will never sell to their traditional customers, but demonstrates that they realise that to make money they must make more less-expensive cars as the market in hand-built toys for the rich recedes.

But if the would-be rugged individualist finds his choice becoming limited, the man-in-the-street has never had it so good in terms of what he can buy in the way of a mass-produced automobile, even if it costs a lot more money than it used to. What used to be 'extras' are now commonly part of the standard package, and the Japanese in particular have scored by throwing in everything including the radio into the showroom specification of the car. This is a logical development—if we look back to the beginning, we had to pay extra for our spare wheel, lights and all the essentials—as we now regard them as extras to the standard specification.

opposite, bottom
How old is the Oldsmobile? In spite of its 1920s looks this Roadster goes right back to 1909, when it was turning heads around Detroit

below
Panther's De Ville was inspired by Ettore Bugatti's Royale. It has a Jaguar V12 engine, and everything else—including the price—is outsize too. Not good for shopping

above
A brave British try from long ago, the 1932 Burney Streamline, which like the Chrysler Airflow made nobody rich, and revolted many

left
A German way to make Strength Through Joy. Small door openings kept the frame of the Mercedes 300SL strong. It is said they dropped the gullwing doors when Ava Gardner inverted one and couldn't get out

Apart from all the equipment which we now look to find as part of the package, the package itself has improved out of all recognition in most respects—ride, performance, economy, durability, convenience, servicing. Although we all wallow in nostalgia and say 'they don't build 'em like that any more', if we took the trouble to turn up a few figures we would realise that the modern small car has moved on a long way.

below
Last car of a famous line. The 24CT was the final Panhard model before one of the oldest names in motoring history was integrated into the Citroën company

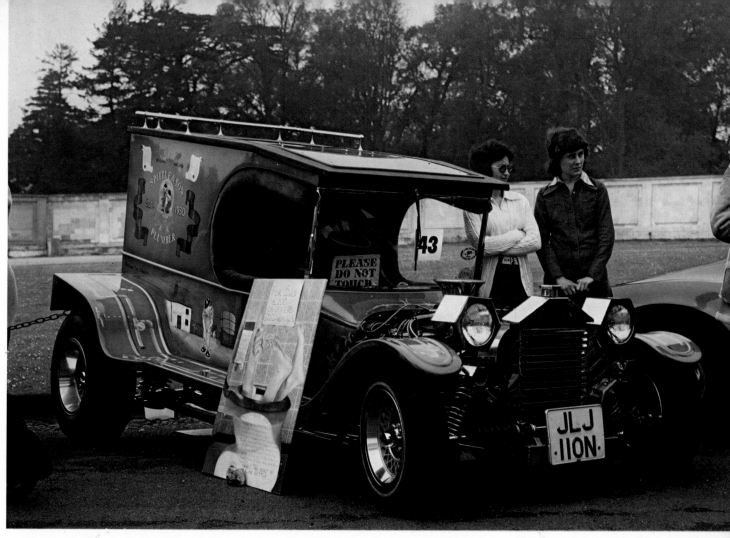

The spread of popular motoring has been the cause, as without the big sales and turnover the car makers cannot afford the research and investment in new machinery which makes it all possible. The fastest speed ever recorded on a public road may have been done a long time ago by Mercedes in 1938 with 268·9 miles an hour, but this bears no relation to everyday usage of the 250 million or so cars in service.

We took a look earlier at the Austin Seven, the Model T and the Volkswagen, all landmarks along the road of motoring history, but other innovators who brought the car to the common man were perhaps not given their due mead of recognition. The general advent of the closed car in the 1920s was the turn of the tide, when ladies no longer needed to dress up in special clothing and 'go motoring', but could begin to use the motor car as a means of transport in their daily lives. The American Budd, who had the idea of a pressed-steel body which was taken up by Citroën in 1925, and then by Morris in England, must take credit for beginning the move to popularize the motor vehicle to a wider circle of people.

Credit has been given to William Morris who did so much to spread the motor car to the British people (and make his fortune at the same time) but many of the great names who were doing the same thing across the Atlantic are forgotten. The 1920s was the bad time on that side of the water, and by 1926 there were more bankrupts than survivors. Some of the great names have survived from the beginning, like Cadillac, Chrysler, Chevrolet, Ford, but dozens more have gone with Dorris, Kissel, Moon, Chandler, Hupmobile, Essex, Cleveland, and much more recently Studebaker.

above
Picture was shot at a Fun Car Rally, and following one of the fun-car traditions, this creation has a vague Model T air about it—or it could be the original Yellow Submarine

opposite, top
Two 'old' Bentleys which are brand-new, and based on Mk VI chassis. On left is the Syd Lawrence Special with a 4½-litre Mk VI engine; the other monster is the Bentley Donington, with a 6.2-litre V8 out of an S2. Bodies on both are aluminium and fibreglass cocktails

In the who-did-what list of honours it is easy to pin down the specialities of Otto, Daimler, Benz, Panhard, Renault and prove that it was the French and the Germans who must take the lion's share of the early credits. America was a late starter because it is such a big country and for a long time had worse roads than Europe, but once American ingenuity began to be applied they out-ran us in many aspects of the manufacture and use of the new device, particularly in the introduction of flow-production and easier ways of getting things done.

Although the automobile was in widespread use right around the backwoods from the days of the Model T, it was inventions like automatic transmission which really made the car the tool for all, skilled or not, and this was an all-American invention. Admittedly Lanchester and others had produced prototypes back in the dawn of motoring, but the modern version was a cheap to make and usable device which did not need to be cosseted.

The Jeep, which was born of the Second World War, must have been the first motor-vehicle driven by thousands of men. Simple, rugged and practical, it is still what a large part of the world needs today, and lives on in spirit in the basic transportation vehicles being sold in the under-developed countries by the major American motor makers today.

In France the Renault 4 and the Citroën 2CV brought motoring to the millions in the post-war period, and the latter curiosity has taken on the role of the old Model T perhaps in going on and on far beyond any original concept of the designer, now given a new lease of life by the fuel situation and the economic climate. It must be out of date by any criterion, yet shows no sign of losing popularity – quite the reverse, and must be one of the few Citroën models ever to make a profit.

Citroën SM was a product of the brief alliance between the French company and Maserati, using a Maserati 2.7-litre V6 engine (driving through the front wheels) in a sleek Citroën body shell to produce a high-performance *grand routier*

Once the world had discarded the curiosities and eccentricities like the cycle-car and three-wheeler (with due applogies to the still-successful Reliant Robin in England), the world-wide pattern became so similar, the basic difference being only in size. If we look at the cars which sold in large numbers before the advent of the Mini and its successors and imitators they are much out of the same mould. All the technical innovation, use of new materials, getting more out of less in terms of power and space, is recent in the mass-produced car. Admittedly all the devices, like the overhead camshaft and virtually anything one cares to name, were invented in the very early days, but then ousted by the cheap-to-make so that we have tended to have front engines driving rear wheels by classical methods.

In the motor-racing world it has of course been another story, and not strictly relevant to the popular motoring movement, and many of the devices perfected in competition, like fuel injection and transistorised ignition, are found on the small-production expensive cars rather than on the mass models, which soldier on with the same old equipment refined and modified to give better results. Then there begins the contrary process exemplified by Ford on their new Fiesta small car, where they have found they can produce more power from a pushrod engine than some competitors with an ohc engine, so see no reason to add complication and expense of manufacture. The constant interplay in the field of technical development, and particularly in cheaper ways of making things, is not of much interest to the man in the street and unknown to him, but brings benefits to the user in the end.

Decade of Change

opposite, top
Volvos are getting more like tanks, big and safe, but unexciting which is the way we will all have to go as the bureaucratic grip tightens on the throat of the public. This is the 244GL

opposite, centre, left
Peugeot 304 is a front-wheel drive small car built to the high standards which this relatively small company has maintained since it was formed in 1889

opposite, centre, right
Renault followed a general European trend towards small front-wheel drive cars in their 4 and 5 series, typified by their 5TS of 1975

opposite, bottom
America's way is still the outsize monster, exemplified by this 1976 Pontiac Firebird Trans Am which meets all the regulations but is as full of bulges as Miss World

Almost any spell of ten years since the motor car was born in 1885 can be taken as a specimen and by specious means one can 'prove' that it was the decade of the greatest change or advance in the history of the horseless carriage. The strangest aspect is how little things have changed in basics in all those years, although there has been continuous refinement. Yet we are still using the same fuel, cooling agent, type of engine, transmission, pneumatic tyres, seating, windows, friction brakes, and one could equally well take the other line and 'prove' that nothing has changed in essence at all.

The proof of the pudding would be to drive a very early car with virtually the same specification in general terms as a modern one, and draw up a list of comparisons. The idea could be extended to take cars at intervals of ten years from the beginning and go through a full road-test procedure, which would produce some fascinating evidence of just when important changes did make themselves felt.

But whatever we may deduce from the past there is no doubt that the 1970s have produced more important advances in the vehicle which the average man in the street uses than any previous decade. Many of these may be behind the scenes development in production methods of which he may be completely unaware and in no way interested in, yet if the major manufacturers were not investing enormous sums in research and development the cost of his car would be rising even faster than the present horrific rate. It is a treadmill process of marching forward in order to stand still where cost is concerned.

Two prime examples spring to mind. One is that of the Ford Fiesta, which in 1976 brought the Ford Motor Company into a market which they have scorned for all these years. They have invested £150 million directly and £400 million indirectly to bring this little animal to market. British Leyland name £200 million as the sum they are putting into their replacement for the Mini which forced Ford's hand into the till to compete with them. Ford admit that they bought a Mini years ago and took it apart, and then decided there was no way they could make money out of such a thing, after costing each and every bit. Now by a combination of cost accountancy and engineering it has suddenly become feasible. These great sums of money quoted in millions of pounds may be worked out in the public relations departments, but they do reflect, even if slightly fanciful, the proportions of the investment in new premises, plant and facilities needed to cope with the mammoth output needed to make such a venture a success.

Ford began playing with minicars in 1953, so that this project has been more than 20 years in the pipeline before the final product emerged. Normally about five years is the gestation period, but this one was extended because the company went on turning the mini idea down for most of the period, although still experimenting. What changed their minds is the very point from which we started, namely that by making enormous numbers what had been considered unprofitable suddenly became viable. This change was brought about by the formation of Ford of Europe, and also fits our period to an apposite T, as their planning on a European basis instead of as Ford of Britain began in 1970, although the international company was formed in 1968.

If we then move to the end of the decade, the Ford forecast was that by 1980 one-third of the total European market will be made up of what they call super-minis, that is cars of the Fiesta/Fiat 128 size with more refinement than the original 1959 Mini. To emphasize the point, sales in this class in Europe in 1975 were over two million cars, or twice the production of the entire British motor industry.

The increase in the world price of oil and the general economic picture, about which we are all tired of hearing, has dictated the shape of cars to come except in the United States, where the size of the country and distances to be covered, cheaper petrol, and high incomes have so far excluded this vast community from the effects felt in the rest of the world. Without resorting to wearisome tables of performance there is no doubt that today's car of, say 1100 cc will do what called for one with a 50 per cent bigger engine at the start of the decade, and this is the class which will dominate sales in future years.

above
Rover's long-awaited 3500 confuses the issue by having the same name as its inferior predecessor which was slower and in an older idiom

opposite, top
Ford claim the Fiesta is the most modern car of the 1970s, although it took them more than 20 years to catch up with the Mini idea. They call it a Super-Mini with more civilisation and space

opposite, lower
Jaguar's fast and silent XJ-S is ultimate transport, and is paired here with a Mercedes 450 SLC, which costs more but offers similar delights for the executive who cannot spare the time to wait for aeroplanes

Servicing costs have also become a very major factor as wages rise, and the Fiesta offers a trend again in providing a self-adjusting clutch and brake systems to cut down charges. Built-in wiring systems which enable a mechanic to plug in and read off faults on a diagnostic machine, already in use on an increasing number of makes, must also become the norm to make it economically possible for Mr Smith to keep motoring.

The other major trend we have seen is the virtual elimination of the supercar as speed limits proliferate all over the world, so that there are few places left where a driver can go to play, or even travel fast on business, unless he takes to the air or rail. As a result we have declining engine sizes enforced by three factors: speed restrictions, dearer fuel, and the overall need to save money on purchase price and running costs. The initial urge to save fuel as a patriotic gesture seems to have burned itself out, although in Britain there are still in 1976 speed limits imposed as an oil-saving measure. Some car makers have been caught out by the five-year gestation period already mentioned, and offered cars in the mid-1970s which would have been most acceptable five years earlier, but had become outmoded by the changing economic and ergonomic climate. Examples are the Jaguar XJS, the Rover 3500 (new version) and the V6-engined Renaults, Peugeots and Volvos, all using the same common power plant.

On the other hand Volkswagen, who had run into the red with their ageing Beetle, have pulled off a successful transformation scene with their new-generation Polo, Golf and Scirocco which meet the needs of the times and demonstrate the knife-edge on which the big factories are balanced when a model change can make or break them. The Golf, incidentally, is known in the USA as the Rabbit.

Not far away another German company, BMW in Munich, have made their success in an entirely different way which belongs very much to the period under review. They began in 1896 making French Decauvilles under licence, switched much later to an Austin Seven copy under the Dixi label, went through a period of making motor cycles and aero engines only, and after the Second World War started in the economy-car business. They ran into financial troubles, suffered changes of ownership, and suddenly, it seemed, rose from a harassed and tottering condition to become one of the most successful producers of rather well-made and expensive sporty saloons.

Then, with the advent of the oil troubles, they made a second switch from the image of sellers of 130 mile-an-hour coupes to purveyors of sober and economical middle-class saloons with a certain flair of line and mechanical felicity. At the same time they derated their 1602 economy model to the 1502 with a less-powerful engine and lower compression ratio to suit Germany's lead-free petrol and are suiting everyone from the economy-minded driver who does not want to go right to the bottom to the executive in the high-price bracket. During the worst period of the German automobile industry about 1974 they were one of the few companies in reasonable health and with factories running full-time most of the time.

Looking at what was on offer in 1969, last year before our decade, there are very few survivors still with us. The BMW mentioned above, the 1502 still uses the old 2002 bodyshell, but that is the only one of the old series models, now replaced by the 3 series. Saab's venerable 99 is still going strong, but they are a small company with limited production and not given to frequent model changes. Strangely the Leyland group's Austin 1800, very long in the tooth, has only recently been replaced. Their unlamented three-litre has gone, but the Volvo is with us yet, although mechanically modified. The Rover and Triumph big saloons soldiered on, although the new Rover 3500 arrived to join them in 1976.

above
Porsche's 924 takes them back to the way they began, in that it is assembled out of mass-produced VW parts It also has a front-mounted, water-cooled engine. It handles and goes well and should make them money, which is why it exists

opposite, top
Renault's 30TS (*right*) and Peugeot 604 (*left*) share the same V6 engine out of a northern French plant, but most testers seem to prefer the Renault in spite of Peugeot's excellent engineering reputation

opposite, lower
BMW's newest series, the '3-cars' (316, 318 and so on) are an improvement on the earlier types, but share most of the same mechanicals in a new, prettier and more wind-cheating shape. This one is the cheapest of the range, the 316

Alfa's immortal Bertone shape goes on, some Renault models like the 4, 6 and 16 keep going, but Peugeot's 504 has given place to the 604 and the V6. The Americans of course keep up their yearly changes, and most of the Japanese are unrecognizable. Reliant's GTE has grown up into a bigger and more expensive model. Porsche keep the 911 series going, although joined by the 924. Mercedes have the S class but keep the older shape for the diesel which makes up so much of their production (45 per cent).

From Italy many of the Fiat models are no longer young, but the young man's fancy of '69, the Dino 246, has been replaced again by a larger machine which is not so well liked nor likely to be a classic like the earlier model. The Alfasud and Alfetta have joined the ranks. Some British models like the Mini and MGB continued to sell well after nearly 20 years, which makes nonsense of the old yearly model-change philosophy. In 1969 even the A60 series were still hanging on, but have finally gone, leaving taxi drivers complaining and seeking a replacement other than the more-expensive Mercedes.

British Ford have changed both their Escort and Cortina lines, but the biggest change in what we might call the Anglo-American market is in Vauxhall, who after a succession of unloved cars have made many friends with their German-inspired Chevette and Cavalier. They followed the Ford lead here, injecting American/German knowhow into the productions of the British factories of an American-owned organization, and in both cases it has worked, giving Ford best-sellers and Vauxhall some impact for the first period in a very long time.

opposite, top
From Sweden comes the safe and sound Saab 99 in a shape which has changed little for several years

opposite, lower
Front-wheel drive in the modern manner aids Citroën's latest, the 2200 CX, which has many virtues although it is not to the taste of every driver

above
Anglo-French venture of the 1970s is Chrysler's Alpine, built in France until the British factories were sorted out to make it for their home market

The 125 Polski Fiat (*shown above*) and Russia's Lada (it means 'darling') are both Fiats under the skin, but underselling their father, a situation not foreseen in Turin when they built the East European plants

opposite
First car in Triumph's TR series to have a fixed hard top is the TR7, which perhaps showed that the open sports car died of slow poisoning from the Californian smog

Picking out a trend is not that easy when so many old models are hanging on, but one does notice the virtual disappearance of the convertible, still very much in business in 1970. The sports car is going the same way under the safety laws, and the latest version of the long-established British Triumph TR, the TR7, comes with a fixed roof after more than 20 years of ragtops. The Jaguar E-Type has also given place to a tintop, the XJS, leaving only MG in England and some small producers to fly the open-car flag, plus Leyland's Spitfire sharing the same engine.

More marques have disappeared and there have been many mergers to reduce the total number of manufacturers. Fiat's policy of selling factories and know-how in Eastern Europe has produced two new makers, Polski-Fiat and the Russian Lada, who are competing with Fiat's own product in some markets, which was not foreseen when the deals were done.

One of the features of the 1970s has been the hatchback, now offered by every major manufacturer one way or another and the type no-one can afford to be without. It must be the only new bodystyle since the estate wagon, which like the convertible goes back to the horse-carriage days. These popular versions of the two-door saloon which made it a three-door—or in the case of the Rover 3500 and others a five-door—swelled total production from 22 474 000 worldwide in 1970 to 29 674 373 in 1973, but after the oil problem the total fell to only 24 989 659 in 1975.

The United States naturally enough produced the biggest single national contribution in all years, with nearly one-third of the total in 1975, but Japan had come up from a very minor role as late as 1965 to second place, which it continued to hold from 1972 onwards.

At the same time Britain's role has shrunk until she is in sixth place in the international producers' league, with the US way ahead with around eight million, then Japan with 4·5 million cars, France and Germany 2·9 million, Italy 1·3 and the UK 1·2, not far ahead of Belgium with 0·79 million, although these are assembled rather than manufactured.

The other major factor affecting the British scene has been the rapid escalation in the rate of imports from Japan and Continental Europe, which has led to threats of import control as it is

much more difficult for British producers to sell in Japan, or makers of any other nationality for that matter. The importers' share of the British market was running at around 35 per cent in mid-1976, which alarmed some politicians as well as the domestic producers.

Another notable tendency of the decade, spurred on by the effect of imports, has been for car makers to improve the terms of their warranty, offering longer time and mileage and improved conditions, partly as a result of provocation by consumer organizations as well as competition. Some are even covering accessories, long traditionally excluded from guarantee, and even including a get-you-home service in the purchase price for one year. The customer is indeed a more privileged person than he was in the days when he was told he could have any colour so long as it was black, or if he complained about the brakes that the car was made to go and not to stop.

We may not have seen any switch in the nature of the power unit, but overhead camshafts, usually driven by rubber belts, have become common on cheap everyday cars, the alternator has pushed out the dynamo, the disc brake is almost universal on front wheels, and servicing and oil-change intervals have grown longer, simplifying matters for the driver and saving him money.

Safety has become the trendy thing for governments, and more and more countries are legislating for compulsory wearing of seat belts, banning of children in front seats, and built-in crash resistance to both frontal and side crashes. The Scandinavians are great believers in being seen, and Volvo's scheme under which the sidelights come on with the ignition, so that the car is always lighted up when on the move, has been fiercely debated.

opposite, top
The Grosser Mercedes which was a triumph of engineering over the vanity of chairmen

opposite, lower
Is *this* how it will go? Sixty miles to the gallon, a no-rust, fibreglass body, and even a semi-hatch back. In some respects Reliant's 850 cc Kitten is the most up-to-the-minute car we have seen so far

below
The Range Rover has doubled in price but Leyland still cannot make enough of this go-anywhere vehicle for the 1970s

The Common Market has not yet brought the degree of international European agreement which had been expected, although the E-mark of approval, needed for sales in member countries, is creeping in. But the French still keep their yellow headlights, and the British still mostly drive on sidelights, and British lorries still move about in almost complete darkness as far as self-illumination is concerned. Commercial vehicles have been much more affected by EEC regulations than private cars, although British lorry operators are still successfully resisting imposition of the tachograph which will record drivers' movements and thus limit hours at the wheel.

Uniformity is bound to creep in now that 'British' cars are likely to be an amalgam of German/French/Italian parts assembled who knows where, and the two American producers, Ford and Vauxhall, are more and more integrating with their German counterparts, German Ford and Opel. In France, Peugeot and Renault have a commercial connection as do Citroën and Peugeot, Simca are American-owned by Chrysler. In Britain there are two American-owned companies and two owned by the British taxpayer, and some of Chrysler's 'British' cars are made in France.

opposite, top
Across the street from Ferrari in the land of Lambrusco comes the Lamborghini Countach. The name means something rude and untranslatable in the Torinese dialect like (almost) 'Cor'

opposite, lower
Ferrari's answer loud and clear to anything that Lamborghini can do is the Berlinetta Boxer, which hugs the road and has a stupendous performance

below
Lancia's Gamma is the top-of-the-range model in competition with some heavy metal from Peugeot, Renault, Mercedes and Rover. But is a four-cylinder engine good enough in this class?

The accessory companies are similarly international, so that strikes in one country can be beaten by bringing in supplies from another, although this may rebound if the trade unions get together and impose a multi-national ban on an international company. Most big makers learned the hard way during some of the bitter strikes in the industry the necessity for having two sources for the supply of components wherever possible. Now that cars have become so similar in appearance and almost every other way, there is almost more interest for the student of the motoring scene in how things are done in the industry and why they are done a certain way than in the relatively similar intrinsic merits of the vehicles themselves.

The old-car nostalgia scene reached a peak in the early 1970s when telephone-number prices were being paid at the swish auctions, but now the auctions have multiplied so much and the number of wealthy buyers apparently dwindled so that ancient transport is no longer the blue-chip investment as it once was. Another factor affecting the old-car industry of restoration and imitation and virtual manufacture from old bits and pieces is that it now costs more to 'restore', which may mean virtually manufacture, an ancient vehicle than it will be worth when all the months of work is done, which means either that prices will rise even higher for mint condition specimens or that people will become sick of the whole thing and cease to buy. If the second course happens and the 'investors' and get-rich-quick merchants are driven from the scene, then the fanatical and devoted genuine lovers of old cars will be delighted and redouble their efforts to enjoy their hobby.

Another cloud in their sky is the increasing number of restrictions placed on the use of vintage and veteran vehicles in some countries, where they may have a special licence arrangement permitting use so many times a year. This has been resisted in Britain by the clubs concerned, as they see it as the thin end of a nasty bureaucratic wedge which may drive them off the roads. But compulsory seat belts, modern lighting requirements, braking standards and ultimately perhaps clean-exhaust control make life difficult for the old-car man even if some exemptions are granted at the moment, and one wonders how long all the international rallies can continue in an increasingly restricted atmosphere. There has certainly been over-exposure of old vehicles at the innumerable events which go on every weekend, but the clubs still flourish and interest does not diminish.

left
Leyland cars sought prestige in motor sport again in the mid-1970s, although never at the heady level of an earlier period when their Mini-Coopers were all-conquering in international rallies, and with mixed results. However, this Triumph DolomiteSprint driven by Brian Culcheth did win the standard production car category in the 1975 RAC Rally

below
Largest front-wheel drive production cars—perhaps unnecessarily large, although the styling was well-proportioned—were the 7-litre Cadillac Fleetwood Eldorado series, introduced in 1967

American attempt to build a car to fall between the compact and large categories is the Pacer, introduced in 1975 by AMC. It is a compromise car, with a wheelbase similar to 1½-litre European models but wider than the largest European cars. It is powered by a 4.3-litre six-cylinder engine

Man's love affair with the motor car continues unabated in spite of all the problems relating to speed, safety, alcohol, regulations, restrictions and all kind of official unpleasantness, and increasing escalation of costs. In spite of the rearguard actions being fought in the United States it is plain enough that petrol-guzzling monsters are on the way out and we shall all be motoring before much longer in small and sensible cars which cannot go too fast or use too much of the world's disappearing fuel stocks.

The future of motoring competition and motor racing in particular does not look promising for similar reasons, in spite of sustained public interest at present. But we already have people racing in a special formula for Citroën 2CVs, which must be one of the world's slowest cars, so perhaps the old proverb will be given new life and *plus ça change, plus c'est la même chose.*

Whatever the development, and we still after 90 years or so have to see the first really radical change in the nature of the beast, there is no doubt that the love affair will go on and we shall find ways of enjoying our motoring in small but not necessarily slow cars just as much as the giants of the heroic age revelled in ploughing through the dust and risking their necks among thrashing chains, boiling water and bursting tyres.

People used to be hanged for stealing horses, however odd we may find that today, but there are obviously plenty of people who still feel strongly enough about their beloved motor car or their driving to come to fisticuffs over it. That much has not changed.

Index